With warmest
Christian greetings.
Alistair Begg PHIL. 3:14
3/29/96.

MADE FOR
H·I·S
PLEASURE

*Ten Benchmarks
of a Vital Faith*

MADE FOR
H·I·S
PLEASURE

· · · · · · · · · · · ·

*Ten Benchmarks
of a Vital Faith*

· · · · · · · · · · · ·

ALISTAIR BEGG

*Forewords by John MacArthur, Jr.
and R. C. Sproul*

MOODY PRESS
CHICAGO

Exerpts in chapter 3 from "Massacre in Rhodesia" are from *Newsweek*, 3 July 1978, © 1978, Newsweek, Inc. All rights reserved. Reprinted by permission.

All scripture quotations, unless indicated, are taken from the *Holy Bible: New International Version®*. Copyright © 1973, 1978, 1984 International Bible Society. Used by permission of Zondervan Publishing House. All rights reserved.

Verses marked (TLB) are taken from *The Living Bible* © 1971. Used by permission of Tyndale House Publishers, Inc., Wheaton, IL 60189. All rights reserved.

Scripture quotations marked (PHILLIPS) are from *The New Testament in Modern English*, translated by J. B. Phillips (New York: Macmillan). Copyright © J. B. Phillips, 1958.

Scripture quotations marked (NKJV) are taken from *The Holy Bible, New King James Version* © 1982. *New King James Version, New Testament and New Testament with Psalms* © 1980, 1979 by Thomas Nelson, Inc.

Scripture quotations marked (NRSV) are taken from the *New Revised Standard Version of the Bible*, © 1989, Division of Christian Education of the National Council of Churches of Christ in the United States of America, and are used by permission.

Scripture quotations marked (KJV) are taken from the King James Version.

The use of selected references from various versions of the Bible in this publication does not necessarily imply publisher endorsement of the versions in their entirety.

ISBN 0-8024-7138-2

3 5 7 9 10 8 6 4 2

Printed in the United States of America

To my father
and the memory of my mother

FOREWORDS

*T*he apostle Paul wrote: "Therefore also we have as our *ambition* . . . to be pleasing to Him" (2 Corinthians 5:9 NASB; italics added).

Ambition can be motivated by the love of what is truly honorable. The Greeks tended to see ambition in a noble way. To them it was *philo temeomai*—"to love honor"—and referred to someone striving for noble goals.

Paul was so ambitious it is fair to say he was driven by his ambition to the degree that absolutely nothing could successfully stand in the way. He is a model for all believers of unstoppable ambition of the noblest kind.

What made his ambition stand out as noble and honorable against the typical wickedness of most ambition was that it was selfless. His driving ambition was "to be pleasing to Him." He lived for the Lord's pleasure and to teach others to do the same.

> Finally, brothers, we instructed you how to live in order to please God, as in fact you are living. Now we ask you and urge you in the Lord Jesus to do this more and more. For you know what instructions we gave you by the authority of the Lord Jesus. (1 Thessalonians 4:1–2)

The devoted apostle commands us all to "find out

what pleases the Lord" (Ephesians 5:10), and to "please him in every way" (Colossians 1:10).

In light of such urgency in the matter of noble ambition to please God, you should rejoice in the treasure you are holding in your hands, because its richness will provide a clear path to follow, which will lead you to that monumental face-to-face meeting with the Lord Jesus Christ where, your ambition fulfilled, you will find out that all the time it was God Himself working "in us what is pleasing to him, through Jesus Christ, to whom be glory for ever and ever. Amen." (Hebrews 13:21).

The truths in this feast Alistair has set before us are eternal, but the table setting and arrangement are exhilaratingly fresh, captivating, and warmly personal. Because pleasing Him is our own ambition, the *sine qua non*, only the foolish would resist the great help to fulfill this ambition this book will provide.

Deep thanks, Alistair,

> John MacArthur
> Grace Community Church
> Sun Valley, California

$\mathcal{I}$n the flow of history sometimes undercurrents emerge that are hardly noticeable. Like raindrops that accumulate and form rivulets; and rivulets that become streams; and streams, rivers that empty into oceans, these tiny movements can swell into great things. Who knows how great movements begin? They transcend the plans and machinations of men, being prompted and guided by the invisible hand of Providence.

Such was the nail that posted ninety-five theses on a church door in Wittenberg. Today such a small current is gathering strength. It is alive and pulsating, like a heart pumping fresh blood into the body of Christ. It has the look and feel of historic English and American Puritanism. It is bringing new life. It is arousing interest and focus upon the glory of God, a theme that is manifest in all true revivals of church history. For want of a better label, let me call this movement Neo-Puritanism.

This renewed fascination with historic Puritanism has yielded eddys of spiritual awakening that are swirling around the church. To change the metaphor, they are zephyrs of wind currents. Soft, refreshing breezes. Not yet anything like gale force winds, nor even approaching a hurricane. It is a Protestant aggiornamento. The windows are open and the breezes are rustling the curtains.

Alistair Begg incarnates this Neo-Puritan movement, a humble champion who has been galvanized by a magnificent obsession with the God-centered life. From his native Scotland, Begg has been a pilgrim in America. He is a modern "Braveheart," a man who sees the biblical faith not just as something he believes and embraces, for Begg it is a mission.

This book from the pen of Alistair Begg is a chronicle of his own spiritual pilgrimage. Reading it is almost impolite. It is like eavesdropping on a soul engaged in communion with the great God's ears alone. It reads as a spiritual road map, a trustworthy guide to vital faith and life.

Begg is an anachronism. He breaks the mold of contemporary evangelicalism, the mold that has been marred by narcissism and sullied by a preoccupation with a man-centered focus on method, technique, and a virulent form of self-esteem. In this book self-esteem is not destroyed. Indeed, a fraudulent form of it is exposed and its pagan ties shattered. But here human dignity is recovered in its genuine form, cast in its dependence upon and reflection of the glory of God. I pray that this rivulet will become an ocean, this zephyr a hurricane.

R. C. Sproul
Ligonier Ministries
Orlando, Florida

ACKNOWLEDGMENTS

$\mathcal{T}$his book could never come to fruition were it not for the help and encouragement I have received from so many. I am indebted to all who have taught the Word of God to me since childhood—Sunday school teachers, Crusader class leaders, pastors, and missionaries—who by their instruction and inspiration have marked my life indelibly. I am quite literally moved to tears as a great kaleidoscope of faces forms in my mind's eye as I write. To mention individual names from this vast company would be a mistake.

In the scope of this project I have counted it an immense privilege to discover the friendship and to be under the guidance and tutelage of Greg Thornton. Minus the gracious persistence of the personnel at Moody Press this book would never have seen the light of day. To Jim Bell, Steve Adams, and particularly Anne Scherich, I express my humble thanks for their wisdom, skill, and kindly patience in the editing process.

To my colleagues in ministry for the countless ways in which, often unbeknownst to them, they continue to form and frame my thinking, I say a sincere thank-you. In acknowledging the tireless, always positive, vital contribution of my secretary, Kay, I have not forgotten the part played by her predecessors.

To dedicate the book to my father and the memory

of my mother is, to borrow from the words of Alex Motyer, "No more than love would wish and far less than debt requires."

Last and most important, I thank my wife, Susan, without whose godly insight, selfless love, and fun-filled friendship there would be no book—certainly no chapter 4! For never once complaining about my absence, I thank her and Cameron, Michelle, and Emily.

Soli Deo Gloria.

Contents

Forewords   7

Acknowledgments   11

Introduction: The Priority of God in a World of Self   15

1. Spiritual Fitness in a Flabby Generation   27

2. Prayer That Is Larger Than Ourselves   43

3. Sacrifice: Wholehearted Commitment to God's Kingdom   59

4. Relationships: A Marriage That Pleases God   75

5. Vocation: Finding the Ideal Place to Serve God   91

6. Suffering: Pleasing God When the Wheels Fall Off   105

7. The Narrow Way: Never Did a Heedless Person Lead a   123
   Holy Life

8. Intellectualism and Materialism: Chasing After the Wind   137

9. Putting on the Garment of Humility   149

10. Evangelism: The Necessity of Bringing Others to Christ   167

Conclusion   181

Notes   183

The Priority of God in a World of Self

I remember the occasion vividly. The afternoon sun cast shadows over the small gathering of parents clustered at the center line of the high school soccer field. We were there to cheer on our sons, who were chasing hard after the soccer ball. Like a cluster of bees around a jar of honey, they followed the ball around the field, eight-year-olds whose enthusiasm did much to compensate for their lack of coordination. Suddenly, our son broke clear of the pack and, with the ball at his toe, feinted to the left, moved to the right, and drove the ball past the defender and into the goal.

I wasn't prepared for the tears that smarted in my eyes. His first goal. But it was more than that. I had played soccer with zeal since I was five years old. Through high school and college and then evening leagues as an adult, I would always rather play than watch. Standing on the sidelines, I was able to applaud the success of others, but I had never known the emo-

tion that accompanied the success of my son. I had not
realized it was possible to take such an intense delight
in, to be so incredibly pleased by, seeing someone else
succeed.

I thought about it then and have considered it
often since. If I, an earthly father, can know such a sensation of pleasure in the well-being of my son, surely
that gives an inkling of how our heavenly Father feels
when we please Him. If we could only grasp and be
grasped by this, our lives would be revolutionized.

And revolutionized is what they need to be, living
as we do at a time when "pleasing ourselves" is the cre-
do of our culture. On my desk as I write is the cover
story of *Sports Illustrated*, featuring a famous athlete,
who is described as "a rare human with both the posi-
tioning and the resolve to live by his own rules and
attack life without regard to the demands or plans or
standards imposed by others." His excessive behavior
may make him rare, but the basic philosophy of life
that puts "me first" is more common in our culture and
in our churches than we care to admit.

Consider the preoccupation so many have with
finding a church that will "meet their needs," matched
by the feverish attempt of many churches to find out
what their "customers" want and then to supply it. And
what about the almost wholesale acceptance of the
notion that learning how to love ourselves is the key to
loving God and others? What the apostle Paul described
to Timothy as an essential problem—"in the last days

[people] will be lovers of themselves" (2 Timothy 3:1–2)—has come to be seen as a solution. How different this is from the perspective of John Calvin: "Man never achieves a clear knowledge of himself unless he has first looked upon God's face, and then descends from contemplating Him to scrutinize himself."

In the seventeenth century, Lewis Bayly, the bishop of Bangor and chaplain to the king of England, wrote a book entitled *The Practice of Piety: Directing a Christian How to Walk that He May Please God*. It went through seventy-one English editions by 1792 and was also translated into most European languages, including Dutch, French, German, and Polish. The bookshelves of believers in the seventeenth and eighteenth centuries held copies not only of the Bible and *The Pilgrim's Progress* but also of this universally read book of devotion. The Puritans of New England even translated it into the Indian language used in Massachusetts (1665). The emphasis of this book is one that might not be so popular today. Pleasing God, Bayly argues, is not a matter of personal choice, but an imperative to be taken seriously by every Christian.

Bayly begins by asserting the seriousness of the matter. "Whoever thou art that lookest into this book, never undertake to read it, unless thou first resolvest to become from thine heart an unfeigned Practitioner of Piety." If we are going to discover what it means to please God, we must come to a knowledge of God's majesty and man's misery. In doing so, we will face

God's holiness and perfection and His Law, through which we become conscious of our sin. Our misery consists of this, that we have broken God's law and cannot please Him by even our best efforts.

Only when we acknowledge the gravity of our condition—that we are suffering from a terminal condition the Bible calls sin—will we understand our need of a Savior. We will never come to know the Lord Jesus Christ as a reality until we see Him as a necessity. It is only then that we who are by nature "objects of His wrath" might be declared righteous in His sight.

The apostle Paul describes this transaction by which the penitent sinner is justified freely by God's grace: "For it is by grace you have been saved, through faith—and this not from yourselves, it is the gift of God—not by works, so that no one can boast" (Ephesians 2:8–9). In the next verse, Paul declares that the believer now proceeds to discover and do the good works which God has planned for him to do.

The writer of the epistle to the Hebrews prays that the Lord Jesus will equip his readers "with everything good for doing His will, and . . . work in us what is pleasing to him" (Hebrews 13:21). It is not that we are left alone to try to find some way to please a demanding father. Rather, our heavenly Father enables us to seek and to do that which pleases Him, and if we might say so, He loves it when we do well. This perspective is far removed from the legalism of the Pharisee or the self-centeredness of the child who seeks to please his father by going "one up" on his siblings and drawing attention to himself. Instead it is the wonderful freedom found in knowing that we are "accepted in the beloved" (Ephesians 1:6 KJV) and that our heavenly Father chooses to take pleasure in our approaches and our achievements, no matter how minor or insignificant they may appear to others.

In the film *Chariots of Fire* there is a memorable scene involving Eric Liddell and his sister, Jenny. She is chiding him for what she regards as his divided loyalty between his athletics and his commitment to Christ. She reminds him that God made him for Himself. He replies: "Aye, Jenny, I know, but he also made me fast, and when I run, I feel His pleasure." For us, this may not be athletics. It may be accounting or selling or teaching or nursing or mothering. In the latter case, this would allow a mother to declare with conviction: "And when I make the lunches, I feel His pleasure."

The psalmist reminds us that the Lord takes pleasure in "those who fear him, who put their hope in his unfailing love" (Psalm 147:11). We make a great mistake if we think of doing this as a compartment of life marked "spiritual," or "religious," rather than as a total way of life involving pleasing God in all its aspects. We want to learn to be able to say with Paul, "We make it our goal to please him" (2 Corinthians 5:9).

In this book we are looking at the subject of pleasing God in light of putting God first, spiritual fitness, prayer, sacrifice, relationships, vocation, suffering, the heedful life, intellectualism and materialism, humility, and evangelism. The list is not exhaustive. It is selective and represents something of my own spiritual pilgrimage. In a world of self, we need to give way to the priority of God and to "find out what pleases the Lord" (Ephesians 5:10). The Bible confronts us with divine obligation, and we cannot set aside His Law in deference to merely human suggestions or ideas. John Stott writes: "Our acceptance before God is *not* due to our observance of the law, but as Christians we are still under obligation to keep God's moral law and commandments. . . . The purpose of the Holy Spirit's dwelling in our heart is that he might write God's law there."[1]

The Lord Jesus declared, "I always do what pleases Him" (John 8:29). If the focus of Jesus' ministry was on pleasing His Father, we surely can do nothing other than to seek to follow in His steps.

FRUITFUL LIVING

The apostle Paul tells the Colossian believers that four common threads must be woven into the fabric of our lives as expressions of a life that pleases Him "in every way" (Colossians 1:10).

The first of these threads is fruitful living. The radical transformation whereby we who "were dead in transgressions" were "made . . . alive" with Christ is described in a variety of ways in the New Testament

(Ephesians 2:5). Our lives were formerly characterized by the fruitless deeds of darkness, and now we have become fruitful. In Ephesians 5, Paul describes this fruitfulness as "goodness, righteousness and truth" (v. 9). God is pleased by our goodness. In his short letter to Titus, Paul emphasizes this point. The older women, by precept and practice, should "teach what is good" (Titus 2:3). Titus should impact the young men "by doing what is good" (v. 7). The people of God should be eager to do what is good and careful to devote themselves to that end. Although the Gospel is theological in its foundations, it is ethical in its implications. This fruit is produced in our lives not by human endeavor but by the Holy Spirit.

KNOWLEDGEABLE LIVING

That this is a process is clear from the text "Growing in the knowledge of God"(Colossians 1:10). At the time Paul wrote, there were those who held out the possibility of a mysterious knowledge of God available only to a certain few who were initiated in the pathways of the false teachers. Today, a growing body of literature in the secular bookstores of America is given over to some kind of knowledge of God. The knowledge Paul is referring to is part of the birthright of all who are in Christ. We are not to be led astray by superficial theories or secretive heresies but instead must understand that Christianity is not served by mindlessness, but by the knowledge of God through the Word of God. Such a knowledge engages our minds, stirs our hearts, and transforms our lives.

This knowledge is personal. How is it fostered? By listening to what He says (the priority of preaching), by engaging Him in conversation (the emphasis on prayer), by spending time in His company (the need for a devotional life), and by being with others who know Him too (the need for gathered worship). This knowledge is progressive and dynamic, not static. At the end of our journey, we should still be exclaiming with Paul: "I want to know Christ" (see 1 Corinthians 2:2).

POWERFUL LIVING

If we are to please God in every way, we need a power beyond ourselves. We need divine resources to meet the demands of Christian service. Neither aspiration, perspiration, nor determination will be adequate for the challenge. What is required is inspiration—the inbreathing of power from God. This reception of divine enabling is, according to Paul, a present continuous experience. It is not like being a human cannonball—experiencing a great initial surge of power followed by the awareness of being on one's own. Instead, the biblical picture is one of a steady enduement of power that is sufficient for the journey.

This power is discovered in God's provision by the Holy Spirit. "Not by might nor by power, but by my Spirit, says the Lord Almighty" (Zechariah 4:6). It is displayed not in dramatic manifestations that intrigue men but in lives of quiet confidence and steady persistence that glorify God. It is found in the lives of those who care without complaint for the needs of their failing loved ones. It is displayed in the fortitude of those who endure the pain of progressive illness without succumbing to the temptation to bitterness and resentment. Although our contemporary preoccupation is with the power to heal, we err by failing to understand the miracle of God's grace in granting the power necessary for endurance and patience.

THANKFUL LIVING

God is pleased when all our days and duties are marked by gratitude. One of the distinguishing marks of the last days is that men and women will be ungrateful. They will take things for granted and assume that they are owed something or have a right to take but no obligation to give. In the midst of that cultural setting, the believer will stand out as a light in a dark place by displaying a thankful heart. Consider something as simple as bowing our heads in public in order to give thanks for food. Lewis Bayly thought it important enough to include a section in *The Practice of Piety* entitled "Holy Meditations and Graces Before and After Dinner and Supper." His emphasis is a striking contrast to the fleeting glances of gratitude that pervade our fast-food generation.

Our gratitude for God's material provision is second to our thankfulness for the spiritual provision He has made for us in the Lord Jesus. We who are so undeserving of His favor have by His grace been qualified to share in the inheritance of the saints in the kingdom of light. How immense is His mercy and goodness: "For he has rescued us from the dominion of darkness and brought us into the kingdom of the Son he loves, in whom we have redemption, the forgiveness of sins" (Colossians 1:13–14). An unfading awareness of God's mercy must yield in our lives the fruit of thankfulness.

PLEASING GOD IN OUR DESIRES AND ASPIRATIONS

All of our desires, decisions, aspirations, and affections should be governed by our prior determination to please God. This is distinct from a superficial interest in religious things that is nothing more than a thinly disguised form of self-preoccupation. Our belief should be in the God and Father of our Lord Jesus Christ, who is externally and objectively true, not in a form of God that exists to please us. David Wells says: "A God with whom we are on . . . easy terms and whose reality is little different from our own, . . . who is merely there to satisfy our needs—has no real authority to compel and will soon begin to bore us."[2]

We must ask ourselves, Who am I trying to please? The worker endeavors to please his boss. The child, his parents. The pupil, his teacher. But for the believer, underpinning all that must be a heartfelt commitment to be able to say with Paul, "We make it our goal to please him" (2 Corinthians 5:9).

We may think of the chapters that follow as signposts for the journey of life, or as markers placed in the middle of the fairway of a golf course encouraging the players to aim for them so as to avoid the perils of water and rough. In the old days of camping, one canvas bag, rolled up like an ungainly sausage, contained the tent, and another smaller bag contained the tent pegs. Each of the chapters that follow may be thought of as tent pegs to be driven in around our lives so as to prevent our collapse.

"May he work in us what is pleasing to him, through Jesus Christ, to whom be glory for ever and ever. Amen" (Hebrews 13:21).

CHAPTER ONE

Spiritual
Fitness in a
Flabby Generation

In 1970 a handful of runners participated in the first New York City marathon, which was run on a four-loop course around Central Park. The marathon celebrated its twenty-fifth anniversary with a record 29,000 runners! In 1994 in the U.S., the ten largest marathons totaled well over 100,000 finishers, and well over 250 marathons were planned for 1995.

This is just one indication that physical fitness is on the agenda of many people as we chase to the end of the century. Business personnel stride toward their offices, briefcase in one hand and exercise bag in the other. Young mothers roller-blade with their youngsters on their backs or jog as they push along their little ones in three-wheeled "easy striders."

Technical medical information, once the domain of our physicians, is now the subject matter of animated conversation in health-food stores and fashionable cafes that serve only that which makes one lean and keen for physical exercise. Magazines abound on the subject and carry advertisements for such appealing products as the "energy optimizer" and the "Power Bar," which is reputed to allow one to burn fat faster. If you want to "maximize energy, minimize fatigue, and accelerate recovery," then you should opt for the scientifically based ultimate sports nutrition system. All these products are designed to help the average overweight and underexercised individual become serious about physical fitness.

EXERCISING FOR A REASON

As Christians we should be at the front of this parade. After all, we know that our bodies are not to be abused, but to be fed and cared for. They are the dwelling place of God, and it is through them that we give expression to our concrete service for God. Yet, historically, we do not have a strong track record in this area. Most local churches have had eating as a regular feature of their programs while at the same time rejecting exercise as valid Christian activity.

We tend to be behind the curve in other ways as well. When aerobic exercise, aided by video, grabbed center stage, Christians decided they must have their own version. So they created "Praisercize" to substitute for "Jazzercise." The result? Christians who had a desire to get fit neglected the opportunity to plug in with their non-Christian friends, choosing instead to form another "holy huddle": bodies bouncing in time to worship songs. This allowed them to shun the secular and trivialize the sacred.

We should not be distancing ourselves from opportunities to get to know our non-Christian neighbors but should be seizing the chance to live in the world and let our light shine. That will result in maximum impact for the kingdom. We know that our bodies are like a tent that will one day be folded up when we leave for our permanent dwelling in heaven. Our unbelieving friends have no such hope. We know that the whole of creation is creaking and groaning in expectation of a new heaven and a new earth. Our friends believe that the here and now is all we have. So, while we run with them and share their commitment to physical exercise, there will always be a difference.

We are able to affirm with them that our lives are full of potential. They are powerful in their impact for good or ill. But we also know that our lives are passing. We can share this perspective with our neighbors and help them see the eternal significance of the aging process: that our lives are like the morning "mist that appears for a little while and then vanishes" (James 4:14).

We are jogging with our friends not to stave off advancing years but for the enjoyment of bodily exercise and to honor our Creator in the process. But the striking difference is that our lives are purchased. We realize that a healthy body with a sick soul is a tragic thing. For us, the ultimate issue is spiritual, not physical. "You are not your own; you were bought at a price. Therefore honor God with your body" (1 Corinthians 6:19–20).

INTEGRATING THE BODY AND THE SPIRIT

Eric Liddell had not compartmentalized his faith, as his statement in *Chariots of Fire* that it pleased God to make him fast gives evidence. He did not see athletics as secular and Bible study, Christian. He saw the whole of his life as under the control of God. That would include athletics, music, poetry, art—whatever we do as we exercise our gifts. When Paul told the Corinthians to run to win, he was not referring to a literal footrace but to the whole of life. "So whether you eat or drink or whatever you do, do it all for the glory of God" (1 Corinthians 10:31).

THE TRAINING OF THE TRUE DISCIPLE

In 1 Corinthians 9:24–27, Paul argues from the lesser to the greater. If individuals are prepared to go into strict training and deprive themselves of justifiable enjoyments all for the sake of a crown of laurel leaves, how much more should we be concerned to run the race of the Christian life in such a way as to get an everlasting prize.

The Olympic athlete "going for the gold" must devote himself to years of preparation. This will involve:

1. *Diet*—the athlete does not merely ask whether the meal is nutritious but whether it is allowed in his training program.
2. *Sleep*—the athlete is in bed when others party and out of bed to train when others sleep.
3. *Hardship*—the training is tough and demanding.
4. *Sacrifice*—friendships cannot be developed and sustained.
5. *Commitment*—financial, mental, emotional—total!

Our pursuit of the spiritual prize is to be no less passionate. We should not run aimlessly or halfheartedly, as though we signed up just to get a T-shirt, but as runners who look to receive the "well done" from our Lord and Master.

People will pay hard-earned cash for all kinds of gimmicks marketed as keys to "the perfect body"—always with the minimum of effort. My current favorite is the belt that is to be worn around the waist to reduce unwanted fat simply as a result of being buckled on. In the spiritual realm, there have always been purveyors of the quick fix and the easy route to godliness. But such offers are useless. The Bible does not offer a shortcut to spiritual fitness.

THE ACTIVITY THAT HINDERS

The writer to the Hebrews urges an approach to spiritual progress that is aimed at the will rather than the emotions: "Let us throw off everything that hinders and the sin that so easily entangles, and let us run with perseverance the race marked out for us" (Hebrews 12:1).

The athlete must divest himself of all superfluous weight. Athletic wear is vastly different today from what it was even a decade ago. The quest for the finest and the lightest is in order to increase the speed and efficiency of the athlete.

In a small airport in Nairobi, I was shown single-engine planes which are used to fly supplies and personnel to the various missionaries. To prepare the airplanes for service, all the "extras" were removed. The upholstery on the seats, unnecessary paneling, and any luxury items that would take the place of something more vital had been cut away.

That is the way we should approach our Christian lives. Many things that are perfectly fine in and of themselves may hold us back from achieving spiritual fitness. We must be prepared to deal regularly with these hindrances. Some of them will surprise us. Our love of gardening, reading, or cycling may actually impede our spiritual progress. Our commitment to our families can also be a hindrance if it keeps us from worship and prayer and witness. The words of Jesus put our involvement with our families into perspective. "If anyone comes to me and does not hate his father and mother, his wife and children, his brothers and sisters—yes, even his own life—he cannot be my disciple" (Luke 14:26).

THE SIN THAT ENTANGLES

One of the key reasons for the flabbiness of our spiritual lives is that a generation of Christians is growing up with little awareness of the necessity of dealing with sin. There are sins to be rejected. These are the things that "so easily entangle us." We will not all be tripped up by the same things. The source of our temptations differs according to our personalities. We must learn where our personal weaknesses lie. Once they are identified, we must be ruthless in dealing with them.

Earlier generations called this the "mortification of the flesh," that is, pronouncing the death sentence upon sin and putting that sentence into daily effect by killing all that sets itself against God's purpose in our lives.

How is this to be achieved? Not by a slavish observance of external rules. Paul writes, "Such regulations indeed have an appearance of wisdom, with their self-imposed worship, their false humility and their harsh treatment of the body, but they lack any value in restraining sensual indulgence" (Colossians 2:23). That is so because we need an internal mechanism if we are to put off the old and put on the new. And that will come about only if we have been raised with Christ to newness of life. It is our union with Christ that makes the new life possible.

The power we need is the power that comes from the Lord, who works in our lives to enable us to do His good pleasure. Then we are responsible to work out what God by His Spirit is working in.

ASSESSING OUR PROGRESS

The most obvious way to assess our progress is to test our lives against the plumb line of Scripture. We are not going to assume we are spiritually fit simply because we feel we are. I may feel that on the strength of my jumping ability, I am ready for the Olympic trials. However, when my vertical clearance of three feet is held up to the qualifying standard, I discover how far I have to go!

Earlier this year I was given a rigorous assessment of my current physical condition. I went through a battery of tests, submitted blood work, answered an extensive questionnaire, and then watched and waited as the results were fed into a computer. I was given a report on the basis of their findings. It was frank in commenting on such matters as muscle mass and body fat! There were five main categories in which I was rated. We can also use them to assess our spiritual progress.

FUNCTIONAL CAPACITY AND HEART RATE

The first test was of my functional capacity—my aerobic activity and heartbeat. The doctors checked my resting heart rate and then monitored what happened in response to various levels of stress. They wanted to know how well I could sustain vigorous physical exercise, what effect exercise had upon my heart rate, and how long it took me to advance to the optimum rate for me to benefit from the activity. They used a treadmill and at regular intervals increased the pace and the angle of incline. It was no problem walking slowly on the flat, but quite a different matter running flat-out uphill.

In the spiritual realm, how well do you think the average church member would do in this area of assessment? Howard Hendricks once described the local church as a football game: twenty-two people on the field, badly in need of a rest, and forty thousand in the stands, badly in need of exercise. There is little doubt that the majority of the exercise necessary for the local church to function is engaged in by the minority. As with so many exercise programs, people are often motivated by guilt to make staggering commitments which they quickly discover they are unable or unwilling to sustain.

We need to learn where we are on this scale for two reasons. First, so that we know *when to push ourselves*. There is a level of activity which, although not harmful, is actually doing you very little good. It is fairly neutral. There are vast crowds who are apparently content to function at this level in our churches. They appear regularly on Sunday mornings to sit and listen, and then they disappear for another week before returning to repeat the process. Their "aerobic function" is flat. They do not enjoy the benefits of a good workout. They miss out on the privileges of service and fail to assume responsibilities which then fall to others who are possibly already overextended.

Second, we need to learn *how to pace ourselves*. In distance running this is very important. If we are able to run ten miles at an average pace of seven-minute miles, it is crucial that we don't begin to chase after someone who is able to sustain six-minute miles. We will be able to keep up for a while but, eventually, will be unable to stay the course, and our average time will reflect our mistake. So it is in the church. If we are to run our race and play our part, we must always be "looking unto Jesus," as the Scripture puts it, rather than looking at our brothers and sisters (Hebrews 12:2 KJV). Not that we do not derive strength and encouragement from their example; we do. But we are not called upon to play any part other than our own. We have to learn how to accept our limitations as well as when to assume our responsibilities.

STATIC FLEXIBILITY

This tested my suppleness and agility—my stretching capacity and the ease with which I could perform a series of exercises. This is clearly a matter of significance when we think in terms of spiritual fitness. Many Christians score well in some of the other categories, but fail when it comes to flexibility.

The issue here is the ability to distinguish issues that truly matter from ones that do not. We do not want to be flexible about moral and theological convictions. The great doctrines of the church on salvation and evangelism and spiritual growth really matter. So, too, do the moral standards set forth in the Ten Commandments and elsewhere in the Bible. The suggestion, for example, that the distinct roles God has given to men and women don't matter is not an example of flexibility, but of foolishness. It is wrong to compromise our doctrinal convictions in order to join hands with some who think we are too rigid.

But it is also wrong to be brittle about issues that are not foundations of the faith. Once, when I was a child in Scotland, our church planned a day cruise down the river Clyde. A great crowd boarded the steamer on the Saturday morning as we set off on our voyage "doon the water," as they say in Glasgow. In the midst of the usual banter and high-spirited conversation, I began to pick up a negative theme. The word that still stands out in my memory is *pertaineth*. The men were quoting Deuteronomy 22:5, and the source of their agitation was a woman who had appeared on the boat wearing trousers. Now despite the fact that the skirts of the other women were blowing in the breeze and revealing more than their ankles, this poor lady was being tried and convicted for her sensible attire. No, they did not throw her overboard, but if a storm had come up I have little doubt that some would have suggested that as a possible solution (like some female Jonah). What really made me wonder was how the men could adopt such an inflexible position when some of their own gender were on board walking around in kilts!

ENDURANCE

This tested my staying power. How many repetitions could I complete without becoming fatigued? Endurance is a key indicator of spiritual fitness. Paul reminds the Philippian believers that he is confident "that he who began a good work in you will carry it on to completion until the day of Christ Jesus" (Philippians 1:6). But what about the people who respond to the Gospel when they hear it preached and seem to make such a good beginning and then fall away? They have been attending church, reading their Bibles, and praying, and then something happens and we can't find them. The answer the Bible gives is that they are either backslidden or false professors.

Spurgeon compared backslidden believers to a man on board ship in the midst of high seas. He may be knocked on the deck time and time again by the waves, but he is never washed overboard. This is true to Christian experience, if we are honest. The hymn writer Robert Robinson put it well: "Prone to wander, Lord I feel it. Prone to leave the God I love."[1] However, even though we may suffer temporary defeats in a continual and irreconcilable war, "sin will not be [our] master" (Romans 6:14).

The instructions about restoration given in Galatians 6:1 and about winning back wanderers in James

5:19–20 speak to the reality of spiritual setbacks in the life of the honest believer. Ephesians 6:10–18 speaks of the armor needed for the battle. The believer needs to wear the helmet of salvation and think biblically about the struggles and difficulties he encounters. John Bunyan's *The Pilgrim's Progress* is rich with illustrative material when it comes to this. As a result of grace, we have been saved from sin's penalty. One day we will be saved from sin's presence. In the meantime we are being saved from sin's power.

The ground of our salvation is in the atoning sacrifice of Jesus, but we should give evidence of the work of God's grace in our lives. How can we tell if someone is simply backslidden or is actually a false professor? As long as he continues in sin, it will be impossible to tell. Paul reminds Timothy: "The Lord knows those who are his. . . . Everyone who confesses the name of the Lord must turn away from wickedness" (2 Timothy 2:19).

Some years ago, a friend gave me a photograph of a runner for my wall. Superimposed on the picture was the phrase "The race is not always to the swift but to him who keeps on running." So it is that our endurance is a vital test of our spiritual fitness.

STRENGTH

I can tell you that my son was unimpressed when he saw how little weight his poor old dad was able to lift. My wife, for that matter, was not particularly impressed either. This is an area of physical fitness to which I need to pay attention. The doctors advised me as to how I might correct this deficit with a series of exercises.

The Christian faith is like a muscle. The more we exercise, the more we build it, but when we neglect it, it atrophies. It is in recognizing our weakness that we discover the strength that God provides. It is God who keeps us strong to the end. King Uzziah of Judah had a dramatic rise to influence and significance but failed at this most basic point. "He was marvelously helped until he became strong. But when he had become strong he grew proud, to his own destruction" (2 Chronicles 26:15–16 NRSV).

The Bible talks about becoming strong in good deeds (2 Thessalonians 2:17) and of having our hearts and hands and knees strengthened in the cause of spiritual usefulness. We need strength in order to exercise our spiritual gifts (1 Peter 4:11). And we need, with Timothy, to be reminded to "be strong in the grace that is in Christ Jesus" (2 Timothy 2:1).

All kinds of difficulties and trials will come our way as we go through life. We are not (as we shall see in chapter 6) exempt from pain, disease, or illness. The difference is that we are promised fresh supplies of strength as we wait upon the Lord. Annie Johnson Flint captured this well when she wrote: "He giveth more grace when the burdens grow greater, . . . for out of His infinite riches in Jesus, He giveth and giveth and giveth again."[2]

SO NOW WHAT?

Well, the doctors gave me a copy of the report to take home and read. They expect that I will give heed to their recommendations. At the end of the day, it is not very complex: plenty of fresh air, regular exercise, and a sensible diet. That pattern works just fine for spiritual fitness too. Prayer is the fresh air, witness and worship are the exercise, and a balanced intake of biblical instruction is the good diet.

Once when I was standing in the foyer of a local hotel waiting for a friend to join me for lunch, a sign caught my eye: "Fit for Life." Here was a rack of brochures offering a variety of resources "guaranteed" to move one in the direction of physical fitness. Sucking in my waist, I reached forward and picked up a few of the pamphlets. Since then I have purchased an exercise bike, used it rarely, and sold it. I have received a mountain bike as a gift, and despite the passing of time, it's still as good as new. I have purchased and borrowed a variety of books that provide the "keys" to health and fitness. They must be around somewhere! But I have discovered that when I plod around the city parks three or four times a week and make sensible choices about what I eat, this unspectacular regimen makes a significant difference in my physical fitness. Fitness is begun and maintained, not on the basis of emotional surges, but on the basis of disciplined commitment, and I get by with a little help from my friends.

Spiritually, the issue is no different: An unspectac-ular commitment of the will to the right kind of intake and the right amount of output will make all the differ-ence. The journey to spiritual fitness is not a series of 100-yard sprints but a cross-country run that lasts for the rest of your life. See you at the finish!

CHAPTER TWO

Prayer That Is Larger Than Ourselves

Our family vacation was planned for the highlands of Scotland. We packed the car on Saturday morning and started the long drive north through what is arguably some of the most beautiful scenery in the world. By early evening we reached our destination. My father left my mother, sister, and me in the car while he went to introduce himself to the lady in whose home we were due to spend the next two weeks. We watched him as he stood talking in the doorway, but we were not prepared for the news he brought back down the garden path. Taking his seat behind the wheel, he dropped the bomb. Somehow the reservations had been mixed up and there already was a family staying in the accommodation that should have been waiting for us.

I looked at my younger sister. What was going to happen to our vacation? "We'll find something else," Dad said. We had no doubt about that. As long as Dad said so, it would happen. But where? This was one of the remotest parts of the country. We spent the rest of the day trying unsuccessfully to find a place. I do not recall exactly when it happened, but I have a vivid recollection of my father pulling off the road at a certain point and announcing that it was time to pray. We were used to praying together as a family, but this was a very specific request. "Lord, our plans have not worked out and we need to find a place for our vacation. We ask for Your help and Your wisdom and the grace to trust You."

The following morning (Sunday) after spending the night in a bed and breakfast, we drove into Dornoch, situated on the Moray Firth. And so, for the umpteenth time, the scene unfolded. Our car was parked outside the home of a lady we were told took in boarders, and she would soon be home from Dornoch Cathedral, where she had been attending morning worship. As she appeared, my father got out of the car and timed his walk so as to reach her gate in step with this rather plump lady who was carrying a large Bible. My eleven-year-old mind was processing the information. Last night we prayed . . . Sunday . . . church . . . lady with large Bible . . . this must be the answer! But no. My father was back in the car, recounting the brief dialogue that had taken place. He had asked the lady about the possibility of renting her place. She had informed him that she had no accommodation, and that even if she had, she would not give it to him because he was, as she put it, desecrating the Sabbath by traveling on the Lord's Day.

How wrong her accusations were. She could never have known just how particular my father was about these things and that he would never by choice have put our family in these circumstances. Now I was seriously beginning to wonder about the previous evening's prayer. Right around then my father remembered that one of his sisters had a friend at nursing school in Glasgow who had come from this area. He seemed to recall that she had married a fellow who was the clerk of works for the local district council. So, off he went to the police station (my father firmly believed that the police were there to help you) to see if they knew of anyone who might fit that description. Out he came with the names and an address. Andrew and Ima Ross, and their home was on Bishop Road.

So we were going to meet some people, but that didn't answer the vacation question, I reasoned to myself. Once again the three of us stayed in the car, and Father went to the front door as he had done on multiple occasions in the last twenty-four hours. A lady appeared in the doorway and after a moment welcomed my father with a great big hug. They were still talking as they came down the path together. She spoke to us through the open window, and here came the answer. Not only were we invited to spend the night as their guests, but their car was packed in their garage in preparation for their departure for two weeks of family vacation beginning the following morning. "Our home is your vacation home," she said with a huge smile. In that moment as I sat in the back of the car, I said to myself, "God *does* answer prayer."

GIVE PRAYER THE FULL TIME IT DESERVES

When William Walford penned the classic lines "Sweet hour of prayer, sweet hour of prayer, that calls me from a world of care, and bids me at my Father's throne make all my wants and wishes known,"[1] we must presume that he wrote out of the richness of his own walk with God. However, for most of us those words represent at best an aspiration, and at worst a condemnation. If truth were told, most of us spend longer each day on personal cleanliness than on practical godliness.

It is too easy to believe that in the business of our lives there is so much that needs to be done that we dare not set aside time for prayer. Counteracting such a wrong notion, someone has written, "You can do more than pray, *after* you have prayed but not *until*." It is no wonder that the disciples asked Jesus to teach them to pray. That request is valid in every generation.

BE CONSISTENT IN PRAYER

The disciples were to learn about prayer, not simply by repeating the model prayer Jesus provided (Luke 11:1–4), but by observing the example of Jesus as He consistently went off by Himself to pray. "After he had dismissed them, he went up into the hills by himself to pray" (Matthew 14:23).

In the Old Testament, the prophet Daniel had distinguished himself as a key member of the government in Babylon, where he had been taken after the fall of Jerusalem. He was one of three members of the king's cabinet and was in line for the top position. He was a man of exceptional quality and also marked by high integrity. The positions he held were susceptible to dishonest schemes. But he was blameless. He was neither negligent, nor corrupt. There was no gap between his public and private morality. He embodied Micah 6:8: "He has showed you, O man, what is good. And what does the Lord require of you? To act justly and to love mercy and to walk humbly with your God."

Daniel's peers were jealous of him. They resented the fact that he was about to become their superior, and they looked for ways to discredit him. But when it came to his conduct, they were forced to conclude, "We will never find any basis for charges against this man Daniel unless it has something to do with the law of his God" (Daniel 6:5). They knew that Daniel prayed consistently, and so they decided this could be used against him.

Daniel's enemies talked the king into issuing an edict saying that anyone who prayed "to any god or man during the next thirty days, except to [the] king," should be "thrown into the lions' den" (Daniel 6:7). So consistent had Daniel been at his prayers, his enemies were sure that when they arrived at his house they would find him praying to God, and that is what happened. They reported to the king, "He still prays three times a day" (Daniel 6:13).

Why is it that we understand and accept the concept of consistency in matters of physical discipline (witness the runner or the aerobic exerciser who declares "I never miss"), and yet balk at it when we hear it applied to establishing holy habits? It is because we have succumbed to the unbiblical notion that to do things out of a sense of duty is less than best.

For Daniel there was no such thinking. His daily regimen of prayer, with his gaze directed toward the City of David, displayed to all who knew him the source of his dependence and the only source of man's deliverance. On each occasion when he got down on his knees, he was declaring with the psalmist, "My help comes from the Lord, the Maker of heaven and earth" (Psalm 121:2).

LET GOD'S GLORY BE YOUR CONCERN

Daniel's prayers reveal that he had a deep-rooted concern for God and His glory. If his prayer life had been stirred simply by a desire for personal blessing and enrichment, that would have been insufficient motive for him to continue his prayers in the face of death.

We face a similar choice. Our culture constantly

holds out the prospect of immediate gratification, and it is hard for us not to assess everything (including prayer) on the basis of "What's in it for me?" Some time ago I was struck by a poster asking for the community to give blood. I had come to accept appeals made on the basis of the dire predicament of others, calling for personal sacrifice in order that those in need might benefit, but I was not prepared for this message: "Feel good about yourself—give blood." The whole basis of the appeal was our preoccupation with ourselves. If we are to cultivate habits of private prayer and devotion that will weather the storms and remain constant in crisis, our objective must be something larger and greater than our personal preoccupations and longing for self-fulfillment.

PRAY BECAUSE YOU ARE GOD'S CHILD

One of the Puritan writers, in expressing the natural element in prayer, wrote, "God has none of His children born dumb." Prayer is one of the evidences that we are God's children and that we have been born again of the Holy Spirit. We have been adopted into God's family, and we should pray like it. "We should not be like cringing, fearful slaves, but we should behave like God's very own children, adopted into the bosom of his family, and calling to Him, 'Father, Father'" (Romans 8:15 TLB).

Something is severely wrong in human relationships when there is no communication between children and their father. I can still recall the overwhelming sense of wonder and joy when I came home from work to learn that our first child, Cameron, had put together his first phrase. My wife explained that he had found my watch, put it up to his ear, and then said, "Tick-tock, my daddy." Doesn't every dad love to hear these things? Do we not gain great satisfaction from being able to provide for our children?

So it is with God, our heavenly Father, who loves us more than any earthly father can love a son or daughter. Jesus said, "If you then, though you are evil, know how to give good gifts to your children, how much more will your Father in heaven give the Holy Spirit to those who ask Him!" (Luke 11:13).

PRAY AS ONE CONVERSING WITH GOD

When I was younger, I read many books on prayer. Although most of them discouraged me, others challenged me deeply. They remain as vital as they are uncomfortable to read. Examples are O'Hallesby's *Prayer* and E. M. Bounds's *Power through Prayer*. When I was a student, a Chinese friend introduced me to *Conversing with God*, by Rosalind Rinker. The author, who had been a missionary in China, describes in the early part of the book three prayer meetings.

The first was held on a snowy night in North Dakota when as a fifteen-year-old Rosalind attended a cottage prayer meeting. She was the only teenager present and was praying in the company of others for the first time in her life. She describes how, like the elderly German lady who prayed before her, her words got tangled up and came out wrong and she was reduced to tears. But she writes, "I had spoken to Him and He was there."

The second meeting took place in China with her fellow staff members at their weekly prayer time. By now, she was well versed in the language and dramatic tones that were employed to indicate fervency. The staff were all together on their knees, united in Spirit and purpose. "But I began to realize we were each making a little speech to the Lord when our turn came." She tells how she would plan her opening paragraph just to make it sound better than the others. She would choose a chair near the bookcases so that "when things got dull" she could look at the titles.

There were even times when she pulled out a book and leafed through it while others prayed. "God forgive me, too, for the times I just plain fell asleep on my knees during those long sessions of prayer. After my turn was over, it wasn't too hard to do."

The third prayer meeting, which she says was revolutionary for her, also took place in China. She and a friend were praying together and made the wonderful discovery of learning how to converse with God. Instead of carefully prepared private exclamations, they learned how to engage in dialogue in such a way as to unite in heart and mind and purpose before God's throne of grace.

REMEMBER THE POWER OF PRAYER

Prayer is part of the weaponry that God provides for His soldiers. "Pray in the Spirit on all occasions with all kinds of prayers and requests" (Ephesians 6:18). Prayer is the avenue for God's provision. "If any of you lacks wisdom, he should ask God, who gives generously to all, . . . and it will be given to him" (James 1:5).

Prayer is an acknowledgment that our need of God's help is not partial but total. "I am the vine; you are the branches. If a man remains in me and I in him, he will bear much fruit; apart from me you can do nothing" (John 15:5).

Yet many of our church prayer meetings have dwindled in size and influence. Ultimately, the explanation can be traced to spiritual warfare. If, as the hymn writer says, "Satan trembles when he sees the weakest saint upon his knees," then we may be sure that he and his minions will be working hard to discredit the value of united prayer. The Evil One has scored a great victory in getting sincere believers to waver in their conviction that prayer is necessary and powerful. When we read the Acts of the Apostles, it is clear that the church was born in prayer. "They all joined together constantly in prayer . . . when the day of Pentecost came, they were all together in one place . . . and they devoted themselves to . . . prayer" (Acts 1:14; 2:1; 2:42).

When the Berlin wall came down, all kinds of

explanations were offered. Most of them had to do with the apparent effectiveness of Cold War political maneuvering. Few paid attention to the spiritual battle that had been fought in the heavenly places as believers throughout Russia set apart every Friday as a day of prayer and fasting. Peter Deyneka, in *A Song in Siberia*, writes, "We were comforted to know that on that day the sacrifice of prayer and praise was being offered to the God of heaven from every corner of our atheistic country."[2] Derek Prime says, "Christians who neglect corporate prayer are like soldiers who leave their front-line comrades in the lurch."[3]

REMEMBER THE PRINCIPLES OF PRAYER

Derek Prime lists several principles of prayer in his book *Practical Prayer*.

1. We must be in fellowship with God: reconciled to God through faith in our Lord Jesus Christ.
2. We must be obedient to God: By putting away sin, by maintaining right relationships with others, and by striving to abide in Christ.
3. We must depend upon the Lord Jesus Christ and His work on our behalf: We pray in His name.
4. We must exercise faith: Believing prayer has the assurance that we may receive beyond all our asking.
5. We must be ready for action, for faith and works go together: Having prayed, we must be

ready to be the instruments on occasions by means of which God answers our prayers.

6. We must honestly desire God's will to be done and His name to be glorified.

7. We must pray with sincerity: God has no time for hypocrites who make a lot of show without reality in their hearts, but He promises to be near those who call upon Him in truth.[4]

CHOOSE A PLACE

The psalmist said in Psalm 139: "You know when I sit and when I rise; you perceive my thoughts from afar" (v. 2). Nevertheless, when it comes to the discipline of prayer, even a favorite chair in a particular corner can become hallowed ground. In *A Diary of Private Prayer*, Professor Baillie tells of the lectern in his study, which had a kneeling pad. There each morning and evening he would meet with God. Or it may be a particular park bench or a spot down by the river or some other designated place of meeting. We will do well to arrange just where it is we are going to meet. My mother, who was very private about such things, would read her Bible and pray after my father, my sisters, and I had left for the day. Her Bible was adjacent to the chair, and there was still ample space for the teacup!

CHOOSE A PLAN

For many, the development of a meaningful prayer life falters not so much because of a lack of zeal as because of a lack of strategy. The simple acronym "ACTS" may prove to be as helpful as any. "A" stands for adoration, "C" for confession, "T" for thanksgiving, and "S" for supplication. We may choose to order our personal prayers around that. When it comes to interceding for others, we will probably be helped by entering their names on particular days on a calender, and then, each time that name comes around, focus on his or her concerns. Whenever someone tells you that he prays for you, it is encouraging. When he happens to mention the particular day, you have a sense of his seriousness and consistency. In all of this, the real issue is not *how* we are praying but *whether*. Begin! How the devil loves to hear us talk about tomorrow.

FIND A GOOD EXAMPLE AND COPY IT

In September of 1979, I spoke at a conference in the Scottish highlands. There I met a man by the name of T. S. Mooney. He was from Ulster and was well known as a Christian layman in the Presbyterian Church. He befriended me, and I enjoyed his company. Not only did he have a great grasp of Scripture and a keen mind, but he was also possessed of a ready wit. He was in his seventies and a confirmed bachelor. When I asked him why he had never married, he replied, "Well, it's like this, you see. I would rather go through life wanting what I don't have, than having what I don't want!"

In January of 1981, he invited me to speak at the

Londonderry Young People's Convention. Just what a man in his late seventies was doing as the chairman of such a gathering, you might well ask. The answer had to do with a particular ministry of his. He was the founder and leader of a boys' Bible class called Crusaders, a weekly duty he fulfilled for fifty years. His mission statement was clear. He wanted every boy that came to class to have: A Bible in his hand, A Savior in his heart, and A Purpose in his life. Many boys had come to faith in Christ through the years as a result of his ministry, and not on account of T.S.'s athletic ability or dress sense or knowledge of contemporary music. He was devoid of all of that.

When I stayed as his guest for the week during which I spoke, I was introduced to what he referred to as his "rogues' gallery." His sitting room had large windows, extremely high ceilings, and a central fireplace he kept stocked with coal. The furniture was plain and comfortable, and a large table over by the window was stacked with books and correspondence. And everywhere, pictures of his "rogues." Some were by this time successful surgeons. It had been one of "his boys" who had performed open-heart surgery on T.S. some years before. Others were schoolteachers, others in banking and commerce, a significant number in pastoral ministry, and all of them regularly *in his prayers*. Prior to my visit and certainly afterward, he had written to me and never failed to remind me that he remembered me "regularly at the best place."

When I accepted the call to my present church and moved from Scotland, we kept in touch. He was responsible for the invitation I received to speak at the Portstewart Convention held in Northern Ireland in the summer of 1986. I was keenly anticipating the privilege, and certainly the prospect of renewed fellowship with T.S. made the invitation even more attractive. But our reunion was postponed.

T.S. lived alone and had a housekeeper who came in regularly to take care of his domestic affairs. When she arrived on this particular morning, she was not met by the normal cheery smile and bright eyes. She found T.S. sprawled across his bed. He was fully dressed and had obviously begun his day as usual, because when others were called to help and they moved his body, they discovered that he had fallen on top of his prayer list. He had gone to heaven praying for his "rogues." He could never have died that way had he not lived in such discipline. It is a matter of great concern to me that the varied opportunities of my life can be an excuse for neglecting the kind of routine that is clearly necessary for the maintenance of a meaningful walk with God.

As I think back on that childhood vacation in the Scottish highlands years ago, I am grateful that my father did not neglect to include the rest of us in his "cry for help." That way we were privileged to be a part of the process. I am also grateful that Andrew and Ima Ross honored the Lord's Day. If they had regarded

CHAPTER THREE

Sacrifice: Wholehearted Commitment to God's Kingdom

*I*f Jesus Christ be God and died for me, then no sacrifice that I can ever make for Him could ever be too great." These words by C. T. Studd, founder of Worldwide Evangelization Crusade, are a stirring reminder that a life that is pleasing to God involves an attitude of sacrifice.

Twenty years ago on a Sunday evening, I was part of a small group of students from the London Bible College who went to the Embankment Mission, along the river Thames, to conduct the evening service. Stephen Brady, Mary Fisher, and I were there. The congregation was composed of street people who were, by their own testimony, more interested in the physical food that was provided at the end of the service than any of the spiritual food that was offered before. Anyone who thinks he may be called to preach should be given the opportunity to test his gift in this environment.

After some hymn singing, which was led by the superintendent of the mission and which largely featured the voices of the platform party (the assembled throng seemed happier to listen), the time came for me to speak. As the junior member of the team, I had the dubious privilege of going first. I began with a weak joke about Glasgow, and my accent seemed to capture their attention for a moment or two. However, when they realized that in terms of subject matter it was "business as usual," I quickly lost any and all contact with them. One of the men, close to the front, unashamedly unfolded a copy of the *London Times* (betraying his background) and proceeded to read it as I spoke. I eventually fizzled out and was swallowed by a hymn.

It was with a measure of intrigue that I awaited my friend Stephen's attempt to communicate with these increasingly hungry folk. He had more experience, better material, and was able to cash in on his Beatles' connection, being himself a Liverpool boy. He was going along quite well when he came to a dramatic conclusion over which he had no control. Sitting behind him and looking out on the group, I was able to see the impending crisis as it developed. One of the men had been mumbling about the length of the proceedings (Stephen is not known for brevity), but to no avail. He had obviously determined that if he and his friends were ever to eat, he would need to take matters in hand.

So, as I watched, he produced from the folds of his overcoat the largest alarm clock I have ever seen, the kind with the two bells sitting above the clock face. He then reset it to go off immediately; and so it did, to the great amusement of the group and the consternation of my friend. He ground to a halt, and the chairman intervened on his behalf, announcing that we would have a final song from Mary before the food was served. And so for the third time that evening, it happened again. Silence descended and the men set aside their distractions and listened.

Mary was just a slip of a girl, fairly plain, with friendly eyes and long blond hair. She accompanied herself on the guitar as she sang. She was gifted with not only the lilt of her native Wales, but also with a crystal-clear voice, which she used to great effect. Hers was no performance. It was in every real sense a sacrifice.

I had gotten to know Mary just a little through a friend of mine who was tutoring her in the language of his native Zimbabwe. Not everyone came to London Bible College knowing where they were heading, but Mary had been clear from the start. She was heading for Zimbabwe, and specifically to teach children about the love of Jesus. And so, when her classes were over for the day, this friend, Obert Murwira, would help prepare her for her future sphere of service.

She graduated and went to Zimbabwe. In July of 1978, the world news was filled with accounts of a guerrilla attack on a mission school in that country. One reporter who reached the scene within hours of the massacre gave this description:

> The corpses lay in a tangled heap on the edge of an otherwise immaculate cricket field near the Eagle missionary school. All had been hideously mutilated—hacked and bayoneted to death, bludgeoned with wooden clubs and rifle butts. The women's bodies were only partially clad and showed signs of sexual abuse. One man's eyes had been gouged out and his back was filled with stab wounds. A small girl, dressed in flowered pajamas, had been smashed in the face with a heavy object. Mrs. Sandra McCann, 30, lay dead, her hand draped over the body of her three-week-old daughter, Pamela. The baby's skull appeared to have been crushed by a boot or club. One of the victims, Mary Fisher, 28, was left for dead, but she managed to crawl to safety in the bushes; by the time I reached the mission, she had been sent to a Salisbury hospital and doctors were fighting to save her life.[1]

Within twenty-four hours we were to learn that Mary Fisher had paid the ultimate sacrifice. When they gathered up her belongings, I am told that they found in her possession a cassette of her leading some children in song in their native language. When it was translated it was discovered that the chorus she and the children were singing went as follows:

> For me to live is Christ, to die is gain
> To hold His hand and walk His narrow way

There is no peace, no joy, no thrill
Like walking in His will
For me to live is Christ, to die is gain.[2]

Even as I write, after all these years, I am still moved by the testimony of this girl I hardly knew. I hope that in the telling of her story others will commit themselves unreservedly to telling other children about Jesus.

THE SACRIFICE OF FOREIGN MISSIONS

It was as a child that I was first exposed to the concept of pleasing God by a life of missionary service. The missionary conference in our church in Glasgow had a forceful impact upon me as a small boy. I do not recall any of the sermons preached. What sticks in my mind is the way in which they transformed one of the halls into a veritable treasure-trove of missionary mementos. Most of it, I think, was from Africa. There were spears and pottery and beads and carpets and manuscripts with illegible script, but my favorite exhibit of all time was the elephant's foot. I'm glad I was able to see this in the 1950s because it would never be allowed today. That foot symbolized missions for me. It involved leaving everything that represented security: saying good-bye to family and heading out into "regions beyond" (one of the missionary societies was even called Regions Beyond Missionary Union) and, possibly, never to return.

How vividly I recall those "valedictory" services. I was not clear about the exact meaning of the word. But it sounded important, and by the way we went about things, I knew it must be. There were evenings at the railway station when I remember standing in the middle of a vast crowd that had gathered to bid farewell to a departing missionary. There was a lump in my throat as we sang: "God be with you till we meet again." The chorus moved me with the prospect of that reunion never occurring perhaps until we "meet at Jesus' feet." That sounded kind of final to me, and in some cases it was.

In my own family, I was to discover, it had already proved to be just such a parting. One of my aunts had gone to India with Worldwide Evangelization Crusade. Her nurse's training had preceded her Bible schooling, and she had left to make a twofold contribution to the lives of people she had never met. Within months of her arrival she contracted a rare disease from which she never recovered.

Facing the prospect of death so soon after her arrival and recognizing the impact this must be having on her family back in Scotland, she wrote to my grandmother, "Do not view this as a defeat but as a glorious victory." Although she died in obscurity in 1951, forty-two years later from Portstewart, Northern Ireland, to Melbourne, Australia, I have had people ask me, "You're not, by any chance, related to Bertha Begg, are you?" In answering "Yes," I have then been treated to testimonials of the impact my aunt had upon their lives. It makes me think of the words of Jesus in John 12:24–25:

> I tell you the truth, unless a kernel of wheat falls to the ground and dies, it remains only a single seed. But if it dies, it produces many seeds. The man who loves his life will lose it, while the man who hates his life in this world will keep it for eternal life.

THE LURE OF THE COMFORTABLE LIFE

This may be the stuff of missionary biography, but is it the pulse of contemporary Christianity? Sadly, no. In a recent edition of a well-known Christian magazine, one of the contributors challenged the theological underpinnings of the concept of "suffering unrewarded" on the missionary field. It was, he said, unbiblical and, therefore, unnecessary to think in such terms.

It is both dangerous and wrong to substitute personal preference for biblical principle, to place pleasing self above pleasing God. But it is inevitable that we will make this switch if we are going to make self-esteem and a sense of fulfillment the measure of our lives. Modern mission agencies are left trying to coax short-term commitment from a generation that knows little about self-sacrifice.

REDISCOVERING THE SPIRIT OF SACRIFICE

The great need is for us to be taught theologically,

not just stirred emotionally. At the beginning of Romans 12, the apostle Paul talks about why we are to sacrifice. The sacrifice Paul speaks of is not something casual, trivial, or optional.

> I beseech you therefore, brethren, by the mercies of God, that ye present your bodies a living sacrifice, holy, acceptable unto God, which is your reasonable service. And be not conformed to this world: but be ye transformed by the renewing of your mind, that ye may prove what is that good, and acceptable, and perfect will of God. (Romans 12:1–2 KJV)

When we buy a car today, we have a vast number of options from which to choose. The brochures lay them out attractively. The standard package contains all that we will ever need to drive safely, but if we should like a little extra to impress our neighbors or to leave the competition standing at the traffic light, we might consider the luxury or sport edition. When we attend Christian conferences, we are sometimes treated to the same approach: basic Christianity versus the power package or the purity plan or the missionary module.

That is not the approach of Romans 12. The opening verses of the chapter are not a call for some Christians to embrace an optional, more advanced level of Christian living, but a summons to all Christians to fulfill this basic obligation. This sacrifice is not two separate transactions—entrusting your life to Christ and then offering your body as a living sacrifice—but one. Not everyone is called to foreign missions, but all are called to sacrifice. What else does it mean for Jesus to say, "If anyone would come after me, he must deny himself and take up his cross daily and follow me" (Matthew 16:24)?

The whole development of Paul's argument in Romans affirms this. Between chapters 1 and 8 he lays down the basic doctrines of the Christian life. Following a parenthetical statement that runs for three chapters, he addresses, in chapter 12, the moral imperatives that are basic Christianity. From deep in his heart comes this passionate longing. He implores his readers to discover all the blessings of a life lived in consecration to God. The ground of his appeal is "the mercies of God." He does not employ the contemporary approach—what it will do for us—but rather, what God has done for us.

In the Old Testament there were essentially two kinds of sacrifice. A *propitiatory* sacrifice was for the putting away of sin. A *dedicatory* sacrifice was the response of thanksgiving for the forgiveness provided. Jesus, Paul says, has by His death on the cross offered the propitiatory sacrifice. Now we must offer our lives in thanksgiving as a sacrifice of dedication.

How do we make this immediately applicable to our everyday circumstances? Years ago, I heard Eric Alexander expound these verses, which he summarized by describing the sacrifice in three words I have never forgotten: *living, lasting,* and *logical.*

A LIVING SACRIFICE

Unlike the sacrifices in the Old Testament, which were dead, we are to be flesh-and-blood evidences of what it means to be united with Jesus in His death and resurrection. Whether we spend our days in a bank or a laboratory, our theme song should be evident in our lifestyle. We should be yielded completely to Jesus every step of the way. We need to make a wholehearted, no-holds-barred, unequivocal, irrevocable commitment to Christ and His kingdom.

We should not think of this commitment mainly in terms of geography. It is as relevant to the bank manager in Cleveland as it is to the church planter in Peru. We dare not create the impression that to be a living sacrifice one has to become a member of the clergy or join the ranks of the pioneer missionaries. Many may indeed be called to such service, but for the church to impact our generation for Christ, we need to have a sense of mission in the routine activities of our lives. Parking cars, writing term papers, pumping gas, folding laundry, selling bonds, playing sports—whatever we are doing—we are to be living sacrifices.

The cross of Christ is central in our union with Him. "May I never boast except in the cross of our Lord Jesus Christ, through which the world has been crucified to me, and I to the world" (Galatians 6:14). "The cross is laid on every Christian," Dietrich Bonhoeffer says. "The first Christ-suffering which every man must experience is the call to abandon the attachments of this world. It is that dying of the old man which is the result of his encounter with Christ. . . . The cross is not the terrible end to an otherwise god-fearing and happy life, but it meets us at the beginning of our communion with Christ. When Christ calls a man, he bids him come and die."[3]

A LASTING SACRIFICE

This commitment is not a single emotional experience or crisis. It is an ongoing process, "a long obedience in the same direction," as Eugene Peterson puts it in his book of the same name. A colleague and I recently accompanied a missionary intern from our church to eastern Europe. Mike and his wife have committed themselves to the life-long task of bringing the Gospel to parts of the world where there is little Christian witness. In the course of our travels, we met with local believers, and in each case when we asked them what they most desired in having missionaries come to their country, they replied, "We want them to come and *stay*." They were clear about the negative impact of foreign missionaries who arrive unexpectedly and leave prematurely. Long-term commitment is what they were looking for.

This is difficult for a generation that has not been renowned for finishing things. We did not finish our vegetables or our homework, and we are finding great difficulty in seeing our marriage vows through to the end. Consequently, we do not appear to be good prospects for finishing the course. Some of us can be diverted from the path of faith when we encounter only slight difficulty.

It is sad to think of those who start well but do not stay the course. In direct contrast, we have the record of Moses, who at the age of forty made his "great refusal." His decision not to be known as the son of Pharaoh's daughter, with all the accompanying status, was not some form of bravado. He was not marking himself out as a pioneer revolutionary, but as a pilgrim identified with the people of God. "He regarded disgrace for the sake of Christ as of greater value than the treasures of Egypt" (Hebrews 11:26). He chose social deprivation over social honor; material loss over material gain; physical desolation over physical satisfaction; the unseen over the seen; and the eternal over the immediate. Once he had focused on the treasure of heaven, that determined his options on earth. It is as a lasting sacrifice that we display a concern for God's glory as opposed to our pleasure.

A LOGICAL SACRIFICE

The word in Greek is *logikos* and conveys the reasonableness of such a response. It is not mechanical, automatic, or glandular. A number of the commentaries illustrate this with a quotation from the first-century stoic philosopher Epictetus: "If I were a nightingale, I would do what is proper for a nightingale, and if I were a swan, what is proper to a swan. In fact I am *logikos* [sc.

a rational being], so I must praise God."[4] The worship the apostle Paul describes enlists our mind, reason, and intellect. This living, lasting, and logical sacrifice is nothing other than the presentation of our bodies to God. It is intensely practical. Earlier in the letter to the Romans, Paul explained what it means to be "dead to sin":

> Do not offer the parts of your body to sin, as instruments of wickedness, but rather offer yourselves to God, as those who have been brought from death to life; and offer the parts of your body to him as instruments of righteousness. (Romans 6:13)

As a child at Sunday school, we had this broken down for us in the simplest of songs: "O be careful, little feet, where you go, for your Father up above is looking down in love, so be careful, little feet, where you go." The song went through the various parts of the body—eyes, hands, tongue—and was a helpful reminder of how we should live. But it stopped short of the most telling truth: for the believer, the issue is not simply that we have a Father who is watching, but that we have actually been united with Christ. "He who unites himself with the Lord is one with him in spirit" (1 Corinthians 6:17). Therefore, says Paul, it is not fitting for us to take the Lord with us into sexual immorality. "The body is not meant for sexual immorality, but for the Lord, and the Lord for the body" (v. 13).

When we are grasped by this truth, John Stott says, "our feet will walk in his paths, our lips will speak the truth and spread the gospel, our tongues will bring healing, our hands will lift up those who have fallen, and perform many mundane tasks as well like cooking and cleaning, typing and mending; our arms will embrace the lonely and the unloved, our ears will listen to the cries of the distressed, and our eyes will look humbly and patiently towards God."[5]

ERIC LIDDEL'S SACRIFICE

All of life can be a sacrifice to God: the way in which we listen in class, treat our colleagues at work, respect our employers, and serve our spouses. Unless we have learned to see sacrifice to God applied in the humdrum routine of life, we will be unlikely martyrs. Those who are called to make the ultimate sacrifice have usually been well prepared.

That was so in the case of Eric Liddel. When Liddel went to the 1924 Olympics in Paris, he was thought to have his best chance at a gold in the 100-meter race. But when the schedules were posted, that race was to take place on a Sunday. It was well known that Liddel would not break the Sabbath, and great pressure was put on him to make an exception for this one event. He refused. If it meant that he would lose the chance at a medal, so be it.

But Liddel was also scheduled to run in the 400-meter race, and that race he entered—and won. Years after his Olympic victory he was asked to explain his success. He replied, "The secret of my success over the 400 meters, is that I run the first 200 meters as hard as I can. Then for the second 200 with God's help, I run harder."

Liddel had been born of missionary parents in Tientsin, China, and a year after his Olympic victory he returned to that country to begin missionary service himself. He married in 1934, and in 1936 accepted an assignment to do evangelistic work in Siaochang. By this time the Japanese had invaded China, and in 1938 Liddel was captured by the Japanese and placed in an internment camp at Weihsien. Conditions were very severe, and on February 21, 1945, Liddel died of a brain tumor. When the news reached the West, all of Scotland mourned.

When Liddel left for China he did not know what lay before him, but his life was already marked by a spirit of sacrifice. He began his journey to China at Waverly Station, in the center of Edinburgh. From opened windows on the train, he announced to the crowd that had gathered to see him off, "Let our motto be, Christ for the world, for the world needs Christ." Then he led them in singing two verses of "Jesus Shall Reign Where'er the Sun." May his example stir us to renewed commitment.

CHAPTER FOUR

Relationships:
A Marriage That
Pleases God

I didn't want to move to England. As a fiercely patriotic fifteen-year-old Scot, the news of my father's career advancement was a mixed blessing. I was glad to know that he was doing so well, but why could he not do just as well and stay in Scotland? And so we moved to the Yorkshire dales, to the picturesque town of Ilkley, situated on the river Wharfe and the hometown of Reginald Heber, the composer of "Holy, Holy, Holy, Lord God Almighty." In that same year an American family moved from Michigan to London, but more of that later.

Whether it was a reward for having successfully settled into a new school which played rugby rather than my first love, soccer, or a compensation for the fact that I was unable to accept the invitation, which had been forwarded to our new address two hundred miles away, to become a junior member of the golf club in Glasgow, where I had been on the waiting list since I was eleven, I do not know, but my parents treated me to a vacation in Switzerland. It was not a family holiday. A friend and I joined a large group of teens and young adults, all of whom came from various Sunday afternoon Bible classes, called Crusaders. It was in Switzerland I met my first American. Two of them actually—Kimberly and Christine, both of whom were from Michigan.

In October, some three months after the vacation, the leaders organized a reunion, and three of us traveled from Yorkshire to Buckinghamshire for the weekend. On the Sunday, we were invited to lunch by the parents of one of these American girls, Christine. It was around the lunch table that my gaze fastened on one of her younger sisters. It all had to do with her eyes. They were beautifully blue and, combined with the purple in her dress, made it very difficult for me not to stare. Because my home was some three hundred miles away, I asked her if it would be OK for me to write to her. And so it began, a letter-writing saga of epic proportions, lasting seven years and spanning the Atlantic Ocean.

There's a detail here that I haven't mentioned as yet. I never used to mind doing so, but with my children growing so quickly, I certainly don't want them using this as leverage. I was, of course, in my mind, mature. Isn't every sixteen-year-old? But Susan, when I met her, was still three months away from her fourteenth birthday! We saw each other sparingly and wrote letters frequently. In the summer of 1971 what I dreaded came to pass. Her family went back to the States for a vacation and received word of their transfer from England to the United States. Susan was gone. The Atlantic was wide, the airfare was expensive, and I was in no position to chase after her.

The friend with whom I had gone to Switzerland some years before had all during this time maintained a similar friendship with Sue's sister, Christine. So we were in the same boat. He did the sensible thing. He wrote a final letter, thanking Christine for her friendship and wishing her well. I did the crazy thing. I wrote to Susan and told her that no matter how long it took me, I would find a way to come to America and I would see her again. In the meantime, I badly wanted to maintain our friendship by letter. The three hundred miles had suddenly become three thousand, but so what, mail goes that far.

Twelve months later I was standing in the lobby of the Adolphus Hotel in Dallas. My heart was pounding so loudly I was sure that everyone could hear. Campus Crusade had invaded the city. It was Expo '72, and Sue's family had chosen to attend, and so had I. And there she was. Standing right in front of me, by this time seventeen and myself an aging twenty-year-old. I thought I had remembered those eyes; I hadn't. I was sure I knew how lovely she was; I didn't. Instinctively, I knew my hair was too long and my jeans too tight. Her father, who wasn't far behind, quickly confirmed that perception for me.

I visited Michigan and met all her friends. The boys I immediately disliked. They all looked to me like Marine recruits, and they took great delight in trying to drown me under the pretense of teaching me to water ski. Nobody told me that when you fail to get up, you allow the tow rope to go. There were dramatic scenes as I disappeared beneath the water only to rise again, still holding on grimly and being trailed like a dead dog. How could I ever hope to compete for Sue's attention and affection, with these fellows?

Then there was the famous motor bike incident. I was invited to be a part of riding dirt bikes in the Michigan sand dunes. The picture was fairly clear. Boy on the front, girl on the back, pop the clutch and off you go. Not so fast! I had never ridden one of these things, but I was not about to admit it and lose face. So, I took my place in the starting lineup, and Susan graciously agreed to be my partner. I should add that for some reason I was suffering from the worst hay fever I had ever experienced, and I was having frequent nosebleeds. Well, off we went. Off the bike, that is. We hadn't gone sixty yards before I lost it in the sand. Fortunately, all of the hotshots were too far ahead to realize. I tried a couple more times without success, and then Sue offered to drive if I would not mind riding on the back. She had not to this point confessed to her love of and ability with these bikes.

Picture the scene. The other couples, having completed the circuit, are eagerly anticipating the return of Susan and the longhaired Scottish weirdo. They could not have hoped for a grander entry. Sue driving and over her shoulder the skinny face of the Scotsman doubling as a native American on account of the pattern traced across my visage by the combined effects of the nosebleed and the frequent nose dives into the sand.

And then it was the airport in Detroit and the prospect of that ocean between us all over again. In less than twenty-four hours I was in England, and another year went by. During that year we agreed upon a plan. It was crazy to think that we would not have other friends, and I certainly knew that there would be many young men interested in Sue. So the agreement was simple. Given the depth of feeling we had for each other, despite the passage of time and the geographical separation, we affirmed our affection for each other. If, however, someone came along who could displace either of us, then that would be it. We would make it known and go our separate ways. Despite a few moments of uncertainty, we made it and were married August 16, 1975. The rest, as they say, is history.

The risk of losing each other was very real and was not undertaken lightly or casually. It was more than a little scary, but in the end it actually served to confirm what was in our own hearts. Learning to trust God and wait upon the Lord is rarely easy, but it is always in our best interest as well as being pleasing to God. This is as true for the person called to singleness as for the one called to marriage. One only has to look around at the epidemic of unhappy relationships and broken marriages to appreciate the truth of this.

There is probably no more practical area of life that reveals the challenges of pleasing God than in relationships. It is where we learn to say no to pleasing ourselves and yes to pleasing others and pleasing God first. But the marriage relationship is especially profound, even sacred, because Scripture tells us that it is a picture of Christ and the church—and He desires to produce a bride "without stain or wrinkle or any other blemish, but holy and blameless" (Ephesians 5:27).

For Sue and me, these lessons only began in our transatlantic courtship and have continued as a daily process throughout our marriage. Twenty years and three teenagers later, we've discovered that maturity brings real benefits. We have been discovering that a good marriage is not easy, but it is straightforward. And it is fun. And time flies when you are having fun!

"PUSH BACK AND TAXI"
THE IMPORTANCE OF ADEQUATE PREPARATION

Flying provides a useful metaphor when thinking about marriage. Great care needs to be taken to ensure that when the moment for "take-off" occurs, the potential for any form of tragic failure has been minimized. It is for this reason that the cabin crew work hard to ensure that all that carry-on baggage is safely stowed in the overhead bin or under the seat in front. Only the foolish ignore the safety instructions. Not only do they place themselves at risk but also their traveling companions. Part of the responsibility of parenting is to prepare our children for "take-off." There is the day they take off in the car on their own for the first time. The day when they take off for college or to begin work in another city. But the ultimate "take-off" about which the Bible speaks is when they, in the phraseology of the King James Bible, leave their parents and "cleave" to their spouse, or as the NIV puts it: "For this reason a man will leave his father and mother and be united to his wife, and they will become one flesh" (Genesis 2:24).

As of today, I find this a daunting prospect, especially when I think of my daughters, for some reason. I am beginning to understand why Chuck Swindoll once said that giving his daughter in marriage was like taking a prize Stradivarius and handing it to a gorilla.

It is impossible to overstate the importance of adequate preparation before "push back and taxi." Along with the parents, the local church has a vital role with respect to this. For this reason we are trying, in our church, to provide potential marriage partners a course of instruction that will allow them to seriously consider the implications of what they are about to do. We don't marry those who are at odds when it comes to the matter of personal faith and trust in the Lord Jesus.

When Paul writes to the Corinthians about being

unequally yoked, there can be little doubt that his instruction is clearly relevant to the union of marriage. There is surely no closer yoking that ever takes place in life (2 Corinthians 6:14). Nor will we marry those who clearly are unprepared by dint of immaturity or circumstances. It is not uncommon for couples to exit our premarital program as relieved singles rather than as encumbered couples! We have found that it is better never to leave the gate than to have an abort on take-off. It is never easy to tell a young couple that we believe they should at least wait or perhaps even separate for good, but it is all part of the challenge of pastoral care.

A few weeks ago I had a luncheon meeting scheduled with a young couple whose marriage I was planning on conducting in circumstances that were outside the framework of our church. It was Wednesday, and the wedding was to take place on the following Saturday evening. As we went through the details of the ceremony, the girl informed me that she was not going to vow obedience to her husband. I probed a little, assuming that she perhaps had difficulty with the phrase but not with the biblical principle of leadership within the home. It turned out that she had difficulty with all of it. Her fiancé seemed to have little to add to the discussion, which caused me further concern.

As I looked into the eyes of this fine young couple, my mind shot back to a similar discussion that had taken place in the early months of my ministry here in

Cleveland. It was the Wednesday before the Saturday wedding, and I was confronted by the exact same circumstances. My instinctive reaction was to inform the couple that I was unhappy with their going ahead, even though I realized that this all should have been addressed earlier. There were too many warning lights flashing in the cockpit for us to be able to proceed with confidence. But I allowed the pressure of the occasion to influence me and, with a word of caution, I went ahead and conducted their marriage. Within less than a year, the girl had found a place of her own and soon after they were divorced.

Now, as I looked at this young couple, the challenge was before me again. The girl felt that it was "just not right" for me to ask her to stand up and say things that she did not believe. I responded by reminding her that she was asking me to stand up and set aside things that I believed were biblical and essential to a happy home and a successful marriage. At that she stood up and announced, "Well, you can't marry us, then," and she walked out of the restaurant, leaving her fiancé and me behind. He, poor chap, went chasing after her, and I sat for a short while pondering their prospects. Their wedding took place on the Saturday as planned, with someone I did not know conducting the ceremony. It is always in the best interests of all to return to the gate and check things out, rather than to proceed with uncertainty.

"TAKE-OFF"
BEGINNING MARRIED LIFE

There is nothing quite like the experience. The buildup of power in the engines, followed by the release of the brakes, the initial roll, the surge of power, and then airborne. Even after thousands of miles of air travel, the wonder of that sensation never leaves me. However, compared to the time spent in preparation and the duration of the flight, it is really an important but brief part of the whole event. Before you know it, the wheels are up and the flaps retracted, and we're encouraged to sit back, relax, and enjoy the flight.

I wish someone had prepared me for my honeymoon. We had a wonderful time. Hidden away under the shadow of Grandfather Mountain in North Carolina, we were able to live the verse from Shelley about which we had only dreamed:

> Good night, ah no! The hour is ill,
> Which severs those it should unite,
> Let us remain together still,
> Then it will be goodnight.

And it was. But we would have benefitted from a more realistic set of expectations. Think about it. The first time you tried to hit a golf ball, you thought it would soar from the tee in a straight line with a slight draw and land in the middle of the fairway. Now, be honest. Did you even make contact? So, in the matter of physical expressions of love, surely every couple wishes that they could go back to their honeymoon with all the benefits of twenty years of practice!

Not only in the physical realm but also in the emotional, there is need for realism. It is important to be prepared for the possibility of a strange sense of anticlimax, which may become apparent even in the early days. The sense that the anticipation was more exciting than the event. The sudden realization that "this is it." There is nowhere else to go, whereas before marriage if you had a disagreement, you could always leave for home and say, "I'll call you." Now this is home, and suddenly all the instruction about not allowing the sun to go down upon your anger becomes a pressing reality.

"LEVELING OFF"
THE JOLT INTO REALITY AFTER THE HONEYMOON

It usually happens fairly quickly on the plane. Noise abatement restrictions often demand a fairly sudden reduction in air speed, which can be more than a little unsettling, unless one is prepared for it. Sadly, some couples appear not to realize that this is going to be a long flight, and they go straight up and straight down. It is not uncommon to have couples come and tell me, "I don't feel the way I felt. I don't have the same sense of urgency about it all." It is surprising in how many cases help comes from realizing that it is normal and necessary to feel that way. When a couple has mistaken infatuation for devotion, they will be vulnerable in this area. It is essential that we understand the importance of burning fuel before heading for the next level.

"STEADY CLIMB"
SETTING A COURSE FOR THE
REST OF YOUR MARRIAGE

Going fast is not as important as going steady. The allure of "wanting it all" as a young couple has propelled many marriages toward disaster. Instead of advancing slowly and sensibly, the temptation is to charge ahead and to try to cram a lifetime of experiences into the early days. In the matters of sexual intimacy, it is sad to realize how many young couples fill their minds with literature that is unrealistic, unhelpful, and in many cases untrue. Instead of going to school on the lies of Hollywood, they would be better served learning from the beauty and honesty of the Song of Solomon.

In financial matters, as well, many allow themselves to be trapped in a plastic world, where they have succumbed to the subtle pressure to take the waiting out of wanting. The flexibility of available credit has introduced them to the strait jacket of financial bondage. When it comes to emotional development, the art of listening, the joy of conversation, the benefit of shared interests, and the wonder of growing together in understanding, things should be brought to the boil slowly rather than being the product of a form of microwaved impatience.

CRUISING ALTITUDE
THE MIDDLE YEARS OF MARRIAGE

It is here that the most time is spent. It is not as spectacular as the earlier stages, but it is equally important. There is no question that flying long stretches over water is not as exciting as watching the light show of a landing in Los Angeles or the dramatic skyline of New York City when heading for London. But the fact is that much of air travel is learning how to manage the long stretches without succumbing to boredom or indifference. Because something is routine, it doesn't follow that it has to be dull. It is probably true that the best of marriages are not those filled with the equivalent of a series of exciting take-offs and landings, but those where the couple has managed to negotiate the long stretches of routine activity with patience, imagination, and quiet grace.

"PREPARING TO LAND"
CLOSING DAYS TOGETHER

"In preparation for our final descent into the Chicago area, the captain has turned on the fasten seat belt sign." These familiar words underscore the importance of making adequate preparation for a safe landing. It is important that we prepare each other for the landing. The chances are that we will not reach our destination at the same time, although every couple, I am sure, hopes that Jesus will come in their lifetime and take them together. Given that we will probably be separated by death, it is vital that we have planned accordingly. It is customary to have made all kinds of financial provision by way of insurance policies, annuities, and other means. Hopefully, all understand the importance of a will that is current and represents our desires for what should happen when we are gone.

What kind of legacy will we leave to our spouses? C. T. Studd encouraged his wife to say a little poem every day so that she might keep matters in perspective: "Dear Lord Jesus, / You are to me, / Dearer than Charlie / Ever could be." His desire was that when the day came for his wife to be minus his company, she would be so well acquainted with Jesus that all her comfort and support would be derived from Him. If we encourage our spouse to dwell on earthly things and find satisfaction in them, then we will make it very difficult to do without those things. We dare not entertain the delusion that we will go on forever in this world. We need to learn to live in the awareness that we may land on heaven's runway at any moment.

"IN-FLIGHT ENTERTAINMENT"
WALKING TOGETHER

Having acknowledged the fact that large portions of the journey are fairly routine, we need to learn how to benefit from those times. The airlines provide entertainment by way of movies and audio channels, but it is often the case that it is best to provide one's own. This is also true in our marriages. Before I was married, I liked to play soccer, watch soccer, coach soccer, and play golf. I had precious little interest in art and antiques and old buildings and botanical gardens. Today, all of the above are part of my world, and the reason is simple. Sue likes them, and, therefore, I have learned to. Her interest and ability in interior design has rubbed off on me, and now I find myself assessing the wall coverings in a restaurant or identifying the furniture as being from a certain supplier.

I am reminded of the true story of the fellow who began to date a girl whose father was exceptionally tall. The young man was intrigued to find that this tall gentleman walked with a very small stride. Then he met the girl's mother and realized why. She was only about five foot and her husband had learned to accommodate himself to her stride pattern because he loved to be by her side and had no interest in leaving her behind.

Every couple needs to learn how to walk in stride. We have established a pattern of going out for breakfast together on Tuesday mornings. This is my day off, and it gives us the chance to catch up on what we missed from the previous week and make plans for the future. We honestly enjoy the luxury of doing nothing. Over the years we continue to surprise each other with special outings, but we do not live for those. We

CHAPTER FIVE

Vocation: Finding the Ideal Place to Serve God

*H*ow did you ever end up in Cleveland? If I had a dollar for every time I am asked that question, I would be in good financial shape. As you might expect, it tends to be asked by people who are not from Cleveland or have never been there. Implicit in the question is the notion that presumably, if I had been better informed, I would have known that there are flocks to shepherd in finer pastures, with better climates and greater opportunity. This is not the place for me to defend the merits of the city that has been home for our family for the past twelve years. But this is the place to address the question of the call of God upon our lives.

The Bible makes it clear that God's call is not primarily about geography. Indeed, that comes way down the list. We are called:

According to God's purpose (Romans 8:28)

By His grace (Galatians 1:15)

Through the gospel (2 Thessalonians 2:14)

Heavenward in Christ Jesus (Philippians 3:14)

Out of darkness (1 Peter 2:9)

To belong to Jesus (Romans 1:6)

To be saints (Romans 1:7)

To be holy (1 Corinthians 1:2)

To live in peace (1 Corinthians 7:15)

To one hope (Ephesians 4:4)

To His eternal glory (1 Peter 5:10)

Even in this brief selection, it is apparent that God is more concerned about *what* is happening than *where* it is happening. We need to be thinking theologically rather than geographically. We must also affirm that pastoral or missionary work is not the only way to "really serve God."

God has given unique roles to individuals in the arts and medicine; in manufacturing and education; in business and politics; in short, in the marketplace of life. We need to view our "daily round and common task" as the realm in which we fulfill God's call upon our lives and not rush to be done with these "secular" pursuits so that we might turn to "spiritual" activities.

Many young people have committed themselves to a lifetime of pastoral or missionary service who clearly should never have done so. This problem has been further compounded by those who teach, without biblical warrant, that every young man of ability and attainment should devote himself to the gospel ministry, unless he can show some special reason why he should not. This is the very reverse of what needs to happen. No one is to show cause why he ought *not* to be a pastor; he is to show just cause why he *should* be a pastor.

THE CALL EVERY MEMBER HAS TO SERVICE

In Ephesians 4 we discover that the Christian pastor is one of the ascension gifts of the Redeemer. The pastor-teacher, in turn, has the responsibility of preparing God's people for works of service. It is then that the body of Christ is built up and grows to maturity as each part does its work. Every Christian should understand the way in which he has been gifted and then put those gifts to use in the ministry.

In too many of our churches, people do not understand that a variety of gifts are important. Everyone wants to be a teacher, because that is held up as the task of real significance, or everyone ends up working in the nursery, because that is the area of greatest need. In reality, all that a Christian undertakes provides an opportunity to commend the cause of the Gospel and build up the church.

It is said that for many years Ruth Graham had a sign above her kitchen sink that read, "Divine service conducted here three times a day." When this biblical principle is grasped by the salesman, the way he makes his calls is going to be different. Not that the Christian salesman provides a piece of Christian literature with every sales presentation, but that he sees every presentation as an opportunity to display integrity, sensitivity, and reasonableness, and, by so doing, commend his Master.

Surely this principle will make a difference to the young mother surrounded by laundry and besieged by her demanding toddlers. She doesn't need to be told that if she were a truly a committed Christian, she would be in China! If she were to receive a special call to China, that would be another matter, but for her, for now, commitment to Christ is to fulfill her calling in the high privilege of motherhood, believing herself to be on a divine appointment.

FINDING THE "IDEAL PLACE" OF SERVICE

Where is the ideal place of service? And how do we define what is ideal? The first disciples, in obedience to the call of Jesus, left behind normality and security and began a journey into the unknown: "They pulled their boats up on shore, left everything and followed him" (Luke 5:11). It is in following their example that we will be led to the best place of service.

When I was in high school in Scotland, the pool of soccer players assembled at lunch time on Fridays. It was then that we discovered who the eleven players would be to make up the team for Saturday morning. I knew I was not one of the best, and yet I would sit and wait and hope for my name to be called and for the jersey to fly through the air in my direction. I would lay that soccer jersey with care in my bag and sleep with it by my pillow on Friday evening. I did not care what position I played; I was so thrilled to be on the team. Today, as a pastor, Sunday by Sunday I feel the same way. I cannot believe I got picked. I think that's the way we are supposed to feel.

When I read of the likes of Amos, I get the impression that he wasn't expecting a jersey either. His biography is very short. Who are you, Amos? "One of the shepherds of Tekoa" (Amos 1:1). Don't you have anything else to add? "Well, I also took care of sycamore trees" (see Amos 7:14). Now, I suppose it is possible that he was influential as a sheep breeder or an arboriculturalist, but it is more than likely that both his task and his means were unspectacular.

Amos did not train to be a prophet, and he was not a prophet's son, but he was specially called by God from his normal and usual activity to a place of unique usefulness in God's purposes. God revealed himself to Amos in such a way that the whole course of his life was redirected. It was the revelatory power of God that made Amos His mouthpiece. He is one of the classic illustrations of the fact that spiritual enduement is more important than educational advancement. He was not ministering in what might have seemed to be an ideal spot. He was away from his home territory and was proclaiming a message that was met with opposition and persecution. His opponents sought to misrepresent him as a man as well as his motives and his message.

He was God's man in God's place for the fulfilling of God's purpose, and yet he was hit forcibly with the temptation to pack it in and make a run for it. If he went home, it would be back to familiarity. After all, "home is home." It would mean security and popularity. His message of condemnation against Israel would clearly be better received in his home state of Judah. But despite all the intimidation, he was resolute because he knew he was serving God where and in the way He directed.

When I consider where I have been in relation to these things, I can only explain them in the terms described above. When I graduated from London Bible College in 1975, I was given the wonderful privilege and opportunity of becoming the assistant *to the* pastor. I was not invited to become *the assistant* pastor because, after all, education and/or educational establishments do not make pastors, only God does. It was great wisdom on the part of the elders at Charlotte Chapel in Edinburgh to acknowledge the need for a time of observation and assessment of my gifts and calling. They did not wish to violate Scripture by ordaining me too quickly.

It was agreed that should there come a time when my subjective sense of call was matched by the objective response of the leadership, in light of the reaction of the congregation, then I would proceed to ordination. If during the assessment period we did not sense this unique, unmistakable, and irresistible calling, then I would not be ordained. During that time I was given the privilege of leading worship, participating in public prayer, conducting communion services in our senior citizens' home, teaching the teenagers, visiting the sick and housebound, and accompanying my pastor on his journeys when possible. It remains a great wonder to me that through it all, God set His hand upon my life and set me apart for the gospel ministry.

My ordination was followed by a further year of learning with Derek Prime. I often wish I could have those days back, and then I would try to squeeze out of them even more lessons and memories which continue to fuel the ministry I now enjoy. During the time in Edinburgh, the elders gave me the freedom to accept a preaching opportunity on one Sunday out of the month. There were always smaller churches in need of pulpit supply, and they were kind enough to allow me to practice on them! At some point, I was told, one of these churches that was looking for a pastor might take a chance on me. It was hard for me to imagine, but it happened.

In 1977, at the ripe old age of twenty-five, I was called to serve as the pastor of Hamilton Baptist Church. How brave and kind they were to give me the opportunity to stumble and bumble my way into the systematic and consecutive exposition of the Bible. We began on Sunday mornings to study Philippians, verse by verse. It was there I established the pattern that I have tried to follow ever since.

People often assume that because my wife, Sue, is American, she finally cajoled me into coming to live and work in the States. Nothing could be further from the truth. She was very settled in Scotland and had enjoyed the stability of living in a place long enough to establish friendships. I enjoyed America and Americans, but I had no particular hankering to live there. Some of my friends who were pastors had left for North America, only to return in a relatively short time.

One Sunday morning, I had walked the quarter mile from our home to the church building and was, as usual, in the final minutes before the service began, sequestered in the men's room. I did this because it was the only place that I would be undisturbed. On this particular morning, someone came knocking on the door. I recognized Sue's voice as she called me out. I stepped out into the hallway, and in great haste she explained that there was "a man from America" in the vestry. I learned that he had shown up at our home in a taxi, which he said would wait for him until the service was over. Sue, who had lived in Scotland long enough to recognize the extravagance in that course of action, convinced him that he could let the taxi go and someone from church would take him to the airport.

I stepped into the vestry and was greeted by Paul. He was warm and friendly and did his best, in the moments available, to tell me *all* about The Chapel in Cleveland, Ohio. He wanted to know if I was open to considering becoming the pastor there. He followed that up with the question, "Are you open to God's will for your life?" I think I told him I was, at that moment, mainly open to conducting the morning service, which should have begun. I hurried into the pulpit and tried to collect my thoughts as I led the opening part of the service.

Over lunch, Sue and I discussed how this strange event could possibly have come about. I traced it to a friend I had made the previous year when he came in response to my invitation to speak in our church for a few days. When I phoned him, he told me that he had been at a board meeting at the Moody Bible Institute, and one of the other board members, who was an elder at The Chapel, had asked the men in attendance if they had any names of possible candidates for his church. As I understand it, John gave my name as a bit of a joke, and Wally had no sense of humor!

About a month went by, and a package came in the mail containing a variety of materials from this church and an invitation to visit for a weekend. It seemed incredible to me that they would be prepared to fly me back and forth for just a few days, and so, without a great deal of thought, I decided that if they were crazy enough to invite me, I was crazy enough to go. When I told John what I was planning to do, he suggested that I take the chance to preach somewhere else also, and he arranged for me to speak in a church in San Jose that was also looking for a pastor.

So I came. First for the weekend in Cleveland and then on to San Jose for the following weekend. I remember that the doctor who met me at the airport in Cleveland was wearing Bermuda shorts. I had never seen a church leader in shorts and certainly not like these! I remember the genuine, warm welcome I received in Phil and Mary's home, and I recall the Sunday services with joy. I remember comparing the two places and concluding that as far as the externals, San Jose was ideal. But when they asked me to come back to the West Coast with my wife and children, I declined, and to this day I can never remember the name of that church.

The Chapel was different. But even after a visit with Sue in November, we said no. I felt that it was wrong for me to leave my church in Scotland. There were too many matters left undone, and I was at the same time afraid of what moving to the States might mean. And so life went on. Paul visited a couple of times when he was on business trips, and on his last visit he told us about the man that The Chapel had called.

Washing the dishes together one Sunday, Sue and I remarked on the fact that the American saga was finally over. "What would you do if something happened to the guy they've called?" Sue asked me. I think I told her it was a strange question because there was nothing that might happen to him, bar death, which seemed highly unlikely. Little did we know that this man would preach only one sermon and resign before he had hardly begun. I was more than a little disturbed by all of this, and, as on all previous occasions, we made it a matter of prayer. One of the reasons I had given for not accepting the call was that I had promised my congregation in Hamilton that I would preach through the book of Romans. When the call from The Chapel came, I was only at the end of chapter 8, and there was no way I could finish Romans before it would have been time to leave. Since then, I had continued to teach through the book. I coined a line between Sue and me. "Anything could happen when I finish Romans," I would say.

It was a Saturday evening, and I was in my study at home. Sue came in and asked if I would like some tea, which I gladly accepted. As I sat there at my desk, with the two final verses of Romans prepared for the next morning, I leaned back in my chair, looked across at Sue, and said, "Anything can happen now." In that instant, the telephone rang and a man named George introduced himself as the new chairman of the search committee from The Chapel. He was inquiring about the possibility of there being any change in my circumstances and whether I was willing to reconsider the possibility of ministry in Cleveland. I recall telling him that from the little I had heard, all was not well and it certainly was not an ideal place in which to serve God.

In the weeks that followed, God worked in our hearts. When we had first been asked, we wanted to go, but felt that we couldn't. On this second occasion, we were not sure that we wanted to go, but we were convinced that we should. On August 3, 1983, nothing but a deep-seated conviction that God was in the move kept me on the 747 that was taking us to the States. I had made the trip on a number of occasions but never on a one-way ticket. Scotland represented the familiar; America, the unknown. Scotland was security; America, uncertainty. Scotland was thirty-one years of friendship; America was one friend 2,500 miles away.

In the early days, despite the warmth of the welcome we received and the obvious excitement of the people, I could not pray without filling up with tears. It took me six months before I could play my Scottish music without feeling homesick. We decided not to go back to Scotland for three years so as to give ourselves time to settle. I did not want to repeat the pattern established by some of my friends.

Today, some twelve years later, with a new building and a new name, Parkside Church, we are convinced that God was and is at work doing exceedingly abundantly beyond all that we can ask or even imagine. Ironically, just today as I took a break from working on this book, Sue asked me what I was writing about. When I told her, she produced a registered package that had just arrived. It contained a letter of interest from a well-known church in a very sunny part of the country. With four inches of snow on the ground here, it sounded quite ideal, but only for a moment. The answer is no, and when they call and suggest that there might be a more conducive environment for ministry, I'll tell myself, and them, what my dear friend Eric Alexander once told me: "There is no ideal place to serve God except the place where He has set you down."

CHAPTER SIX

Suffering:
Pleasing God When
the Wheels Fall Off

The second of November 1972 was a Thursday. How could I ever forget! The rambling Victorian mansion that served as our college hall of residence creaked and groaned as its inhabitants launched their attack upon the day. I was still in bed weighing the benefits of breakfast against an extra twenty horizontal minutes. A sharp knock on my door combined with the distinctive voice of our college principal brought me swiftly to my feet. Desperately wishing I were "clothed and in my right mind," I stalled for time, trying hard to imagine what possible reason could have brought him to my bedroom so early in the day.

But now he was in the room. Asking my roommate to leave us alone, he pulled the chair out from under my desk and sat down. I searched his eyes for any indication of his mission but found no hint of what was to follow. "Alistair, I have just had your father on the phone. Last evening your mother took unwell and"—it must be pretty serious for him to be here like this, I thought, garnering hope for a further moment—"Well, Alistair, I am sorry to have to break this news, but your mother has died."

Nothing in my twenty years had prepared me for that moment. The simultaneous sense of pain, fear, loss, anger, panic, and emptiness that engulfed me was indescribable.

The train journey from London to my home in Yorkshire was like a bad dream. I rehearsed again and again the facts as they had been reported. It had been business as usual at the Begg household. A Crusader Bible class committee meeting in full swing and the prospect of some tea and home-baking, courtesy of my mother. In the middle of that very normal scene, she suffered a major heart attack which, in an instant, signaled the conclusion of her journey through time. I had cried before but never like this. Without doubting God's love, I wondered at His purpose in allowing such sadness in our lives.

The truth is that more spiritual progress is made through failure and tears than success and laughter. If we are to be honest, we have all faced, and continue to face, events in our lives which we assume will mar us, and yet, in the providence of God, we discover them to be incidents that make us more sensitive or faithful or useful. If this is true of individuals, it is equally true of church families. Even as I write, our fellowship is being impacted by the inroads of cancer in a number of lives.

How are we to respond to such suffering? Ultimately, we want to be able to affirm with the hymn writer:

> Ye fearful saints, fresh courage take,
> The clouds ye so much dread
> Are big with mercy, and shall break
> In blessings on your head.[1]

Evangelical Christianity lacks a well-thought-out, Bible-based, clearly articulated theology of suffering. If we had such a philosophy and acted on it, that would please God greatly and would be much to our spiritual and emotional benefit. We do well to begin with the Lord Jesus. Despite the attempts of some to present what they see as the humor in Christ and His teaching, the fact is that He is clearly portrayed in Scripture as "a man of sorrows, and familiar with suffering" (Isaiah 53:3). It is in the Cross that we see this clearly. "The God who allows us to suffer, once suffered himself in Christ, and continues to suffer with us and for us today. The cross of Christ is the proof of God's personal, loving solidarity with us in our pain."[2]

Despite this obvious emphasis of Scripture, we are bombarded by suggestions that "successful" Christian living takes place in the realm of constant victory, health, wholeness, and financial prosperity. In response to this, we are not to pretend that suffering doesn't exist or that it might be instantly cured. Such notions are the product of empty heads and closed Bibles. Instead, there are a number of facts to be faced.

SUFFERING DOES EXIST AND IT DOES HURT

Having grown up playing soccer, I am staggered to see the amount of pain and suffering involved in American football. It is hard to imagine anyone suiting up for the game without an awareness of the sometimes bloody struggle that is about to ensue. But I have yet to see a player remove his helmet and head for the stadium exit because he finds it all just too rough. Yet when it comes to Christian living, the field is evacuating quickly because the players have never read the rules nor understood the game plan. When Peter wrote to the scattered Christians of his day, he made sure that they were in no doubt about the place and purpose of suffering:

> Dear friends, do not be surprised at the painful trial you are suffering, as though something strange were happening to you. But rejoice that you participate in the sufferings of Christ, so that you may be overjoyed when His glory is revealed. (1 Peter 4:12–13)

There is no attempt on Peter's part to try to explain the presence of suffering in terms of sin in their lives, or an absence of faith. No! He wants them to know that those who suffer *according to God's will* should commit themselves to their faithful Creator and continue to do good.

Peter knew about making progress through failure and tears. He had been determined that even if all the other disciples were to desert Jesus, he never would.

He went so far as to declare, "I will lay down my life for you" (John 13:37). Despite his strident affirmations, we discover him filled with remorse and shedding bitter tears, having denied any association with Christ when challenged. However, it was in the period of self-examination and reflection which followed that Peter's character was forged for the good. He was to become increasingly useful to his Master when he had completed the interview on the beach and affirmed his love for Jesus in the painful experience (John 21:15–25).

We might safely argue that the opportunity to walk upon the water, share in the Transfiguration, and enjoy the intimacy of Christ's friendship would have amounted to very little were it not for the pain and tears and failure and disappointment that Peter endured.

We tend to run away from the things that make us. We should neither court suffering nor complain about it. Instead, we should see it as one of the means God chooses to employ in order to make us increasingly useful to the Master. It is from this perspective that James urges his readers to "consider it pure joy . . . whenever you face trials of many kinds" (James 1:2).

Often, we can adopt such an attitude only in looking back. Many times the immediate sense of failure and disappointment is so overwhelming that we are unable to grasp the benefit package. We need to remember this when talking with our friends who are in the eye of the storm. At that moment our presence is more important than our pronouncements and our silences more eloquent than our speech.

SUFFERING CONFRONTS US IN A VARIETY OF WAYS

Peter refers to "all kinds of trials" (1 Peter 1:6). In the past twenty years of pastoral ministry, I have had the privilege of sharing in a vast array of struggles with a wide variety of people. As a young and inexperienced assistant pastor in Edinburgh, I spent a good amount of time visiting the elderly. Some of them were housebound, and others were in nursing homes and, in certain cases, had been there for years.

One lady had been the matron of the Edinburgh Royal Infirmary and as a result of the onset of a debilitating neuromuscular condition had been hospitalized without any prospect of ever getting better. By the time I began to visit her regularly, she had been in the hospital for years. She was unable even to keep her eyes open, her speech was dreadfully slurred, and on most occasions she had to be in bed with the protection bars in place. But she loved to have the Scriptures read, and she would comment in a limited way. She would squeeze my hand in affirmation of the prayer, and through it all she was a benediction to me. There never was any complaining or questioning. Hers was a daunting trial, and she faced it with uncompromising faith and great courage.

Her perspective is aptly summarized by Richard Greenham: "Whatsoever is upon you is from the Lord, and whatsoever is from the Lord, to you it is in mercy; and whatsoever comes in mercy ought not to be grievous to you. What loss is it when the loss of earthly things is the gaining of spiritual things? All shall be for your good, if you make your use of all."[3]

When I read that statement, I think of a young family in our church in Scotland. The wife, Linda, was a believer, and she brought her daughters with her to church. Her husband, Graham, did not share her faith and seldom attended. One evening in the course of pastoral visitation, I called on their home. At the conclusion of a profitable visit, I offered to read the Scriptures and to pray. Graham informed me that it was fine to do that but he wanted me to know that it was irrelevant to him. So I proceeded. After the prayer and with my coat on ready to leave, the real conversation began.

Graham was a nuclear physicist and had a ready supply of intellectual ammunition with which to challenge what he regarded as my somewhat facile defense of the faith. While the conversation was amicable, it was also clear that I was making little headway. So I retreated! If he would read a book that I promised to give him, then perhaps we could continue our dialogue on that basis. That being agreeable, I drove home, found the book, and drove back to his home. Under cover of darkness, I dropped it through his letter box with a note, "Look forward to talking with you when you read this."

And so the conversations proceeded. He even began to attend our services intermittently. He always sat in the balcony, on the side, where he would listen without ever apparently looking at me as I spoke.

What I did not know at the outset was that Linda was expecting and they were very much hoping for a boy. In due course I went to the maternity hospital to visit Linda and congratulate her on the safe arrival of their long-awaited son. They named him Philip. It quickly became apparent that Philip had been born with a severe congenital heart disorder. The best hope for him was that they could sustain his tiny life until he reached about twelve months and then attempt corrective surgery.

Well, we now had a further complicating factor in the dialogue with Graham. "If this God you are asking me to believe in is so loving and kind, why has my son been born in this condition?" Despite my attempts at an answer, I was also wondering about the same thing. Just when Graham was moving closer along the path to faith (or so it seemed), we hit this major roadblock. So we began to pray as a church that Philip would make it safely to surgery and that Graham would come to faith out of a sense of gratitude to God for answered prayer. But that was not to be.

I can still recall Graham and Linda's facial expressions on the evening in the children's hospital in Glasgow when it became clear that Philip was losing the battle. The only hope, and it was a slim one, was that they could fly him to a hospital in England for surgery. That is what happened, and on the operating table this lovely wee boy passed into the presence of Jesus. Then there was the funeral in a graveyard in an English village. The parents asked if I would be the one to carry the tiny casket from the church to the grave. And so I walked, a mixture of emotions and all the time assuming that with this little body we were about to bury any possible hope of Graham ever coming to faith.

Returning to the routine of life, Graham and I continued to talk. Then, one evening in the course of our discussions, he said something like this: "Alistair, I have been thinking about things. Linda and my daughters have professed faith in Christ. Philip has been taken into the presence of Christ. I remain outside the circle. Do you think that God has allowed Philip's death in order to bring me to my senses?" I had wondered along those lines myself but would never have suggested this without it coming from Graham. "Yes," I said. "Possibly. But what are you going to do about it?"

In the weeks that followed, Graham attended our services regularly. Still seated in the same spot and still looking across to the other side of the balcony as I spoke, rather than directly at me. We were in a series of expositions of the Twenty-Third Psalm. On the morning when I struggled through the phrase, "He guides me in paths of righteousness for his name's sake," the Lord opened Graham's eyes to the truth and drew him to Himself and saved him. By the time I accepted the call to ministry here in the U.S., Graham was managing our church bookstall and taking evening classes in theology to be better equipped to share his faith with other intellectual skeptics just like he had been. It was through failure and tears that he was brought into a living relationship with God through Jesus Christ.

These two incidents—the matron's illness and Graham's conversion—are picked randomly from a host of possible illustrations. Each of us could add some more from personal experience. We wonder just where it was that the older lady, who has been so kind to us in our trial, got those kind eyes. Why is this young man willing to enter into our pain and share our suffering? Most of the time we discover that their ability to enter into our heartache stems from the spiritual progress they made through their own experience of suffering. We do well to pay attention. As has been said, "In shunning trials we miss blessings." Peter had to admonish his readers regarding this:

> Dear friends, do not be surprised at the painful trial you are suffering, as though something strange were happening to you. But rejoice that you participate in the sufferings of Christ, so that you may be overjoyed when his glory is revealed. (1 Peter 4:12–13)

Paul wrote:

We are handicapped on all sides, but we are never frustrated; we are puzzled, but never in despair. We are persecuted, but we never have to stand it alone: we may be knocked down but we are never knocked out! (2 Corinthians 4:8–9 PHILLIPS).

Jesus was clear about the price of discipleship: "Whoever wants to save his life will lose it, but whoever loses his life for me will save it" (Luke 9:24).

SUFFERING IS LIMITED IN ITS TIME FRAME

The puritan Thomas Watson said, "Affliction may be lasting, but it is not everlasting." Peter reminds his readers that their suffering is for "a little while" (1 Peter 1:6; 5:10). The trouble is that when we are going though it, it seems like forever. In saying this we do not wish to minimize the daily slog of unrelenting illness or the peculiar challenges of caring for an invalid loved one. But in light of eternity even seventy years is the blink of an eye. This raises the accompanying issue: If we are devoid of a theology of suffering, we are in danger of marginalizing our expectations of heaven.

The root problem is the same in both cases: a preoccupation with the here and now and the me and mine combined with the idea of getting things right down here. If we conclude that we are *now* to experience total healing, unfettered joy, unparalleled success, and freedom from pain, then why be concerned about heaven? How did Paul handle his sufferings and encourage the church to face theirs? Not by trying to produce heaven on earth but by recognizing that for the Christian the best is yet to be. He took the moment and put it in the larger context of God's unfolding purpose, not only for time but also in eternity. This perspective allowed him to write as follows:

> Therefore we do not lose heart. Though outwardly we are wasting away, yet inwardly we are being renewed day by day. For our light and momentary troubles are achieving for us an eternal glory that far outweighs them all. So we fix our eyes not on what is seen, but on what is unseen. For what is seen is temporary, but what is unseen in eternal. (2 Corinthians 4:16–18)

Today there is death and tears, mourning and pain, but one day these will all be a thing of the past.

When I was about twelve, I went on a camping trip with a youth group in Royal Deeside. A group of us left the base camp to trek into the hills. The backpacks were heavy, the journey long, and the amenities nonexistent. But our leader kept saying, "Wait 'til you see the view from the top!" There were a number of occasions on the trek when I sincerely doubted whether I would ever make the top to see the view, or that there would be something worth seeing. But he was right, and the great panoramic view of God's creation took our breath away. To a boy, we concluded that the journey had been worth it. While we hiked, our leader taught us to sing an old hymn, the words of which have stayed with me through the years:

> A few more marchings weary, then we'll gather home
> A few more storm clouds dreary, then we'll gather home
> O'er time's rapid river soon we'll rest forever
> No more marching's weary when we gather home![4]

The point is clear: No matter how tough the journey, we are heading home.

IN THE PAIN OF SUFFERING IS THE PRESENCE OF GOD

It would be wrong to suggest that in suffering we know God's presence exclusively, but we do know it especially. When we are going through tough times and difficult days, we are often tempted to believe that we are alone. While that may be the accusation of the Evil One, it is not true. The final verse of Exodus 2 is a wonderful statement of this truth. The people of God are being crushed by oppression and they are groaning in their slavery. While it may have seemed at times that their cries went unheeded, the fact was that God was listening and remembering His covenant. "So God looked on the Israelites and was concerned about them" (Exodus 2:25).

We discover a similar statement in Isaiah 63:9: "In all their distress he too was distressed." When the writer to the Hebrews describes the priestly ministry of Christ, he makes clear that Jesus is able to sympathize with us in our weaknesses.

SUFFERING IN AND OF ITSELF
DOES NOT LEAD A PERSON INTO
A DEEPER RELATIONSHIP WITH GOD

Scripture teaches this and human experience con-
firms it. The painful experience of discipline leads to "a
harvest of righteousness and peace for those who have
been trained by it" (Hebrews 12:11). When one thinks
of friends and family who have experienced great
heartache, there are some who have responded in such
a way as to become hard and cold and rebellious. Others display a spirit of gentleness. What makes the difference? While both may declare that they do not
understand why God would permit such sadness in
their lives, only the latter adopt a humble attitude and
are prepared to declare, "Although I do not understand, I will trust you." Along that avenue there is
peace, but on the other side of the street there is only
confusion, disgruntlement, and sadness.

God uses trials and difficulties to allow us to develop perseverance. Augustine once declared, "Trials
come to prove and improve us." My son is now at the
age where he is concerned for the physical well-being
of his father and particularly about the notable
absence of muscle mass. In seeking to remedy the situation, he is helping me to understand the vital importance of recognizing the old adage, "No pain, no gain."

God uses trials and affliction to bring us to maturity. The writer to the Hebrews actually says of Jesus,
"Although he was a son, he learned obedience from

what he suffered" (Hebrews 5:8). In other words, it was in the experiences of affliction and rejection and difficulty that Jesus' obedience became full-grown. If, then, suffering was the means by which Jesus, who was sinless, became mature, how much more do we need it in our sinfulness!

God uses discipline to assure us that we are His children. "Endure hardship as discipline; God is treating you as sons. For what son is not disciplined by his father?" (Hebrews 12:7). When I arrive at my home on a summer evening to discover our trampoline besieged by a horde of children, I can get out of my car and offer each of them a cold drink for their benefit. But supposing they are all involved in breaking the rules of safety, there are only three that I can legitimately discipline because they are my children. The cold drink may be shared by all and any, the discipline experienced by a few. As alien as such thinking is becoming, Henry Smith established a biblical perspective when he wrote, "An obedient child doth not only kiss the hand which giveth, but the rod which beateth."

God uses trials to develop humility in us. When Paul explains the presence of the "thorn in my flesh," he establishes the fact that it was given to him to keep him "from becoming conceited" (2 Corinthians 12:7). Is it not true that the prevailing emphasis of our time, inside and outside the church, is upon making much of who we are and of convincing ourselves that we are significant? Consequently, humility is little sought as the soil in which Christian graces grow. If at the same time we seek to avoid the things that God uses to work in us humility, then we find ourselves in a kind of by-path meadow.

God uses the struggles and heartache to prove the genuine nature of our faith. Moses reminded the people: "Remember how the Lord your God led you all the way in the desert these forty years, to humble you and to test you in order to know what was in your heart, whether or not you would keep his commands" (Deuteronomy 8:2). Abraham's faith was tested in the waiting room as he longed for a son, and it was tested in the furnace as he was asked to give him up again to God. What an example and challenge is contained in this single sentence: "By faith Abraham, when God tested him, offered Isaac as a sacrifice" (Hebrews 11:17). He did not allow the questions of his heart to overturn his faith. Instead, he allowed his faith to overrule the questions of his heart. He, along with the others in the Hebrews 11 hall of fame, is remembered because most of his spiritual progress came about as a result of failure and tears, rather than success and laughter.

One of the most stirring examples of the right kind of response to suffering that deepens one's relationship with God comes from the seventeenth century in Scotland. Richard Cameron, one of the leaders of the Covenanters, was known as the Lion of the Covenant, and he was killed in a battle when he was just thirty-two years old. His enemies cut off his head and his hands, and on their way to the Netherbow in Edinburgh, where they were going to display these "trophies of war," they took them to Richard's father, who was being held prisoner in the Tolbooth jail. Displaying the head and hands, they asked him, "Do you know them?" And he took them upon his knee, and bent over them, and kissed them, and said, "I know them! I know them! They are my son's, my dear son's." And then, weeping and yet praising, he went on, "It is the Lord! Good is the will of the Lord, who cannot wrong me nor mine, but has made goodness and mercy to follow us all our days."[5]

What of us? Shall we then run away from the hardships? Deny our failures? View suffering as an intruder rather than welcome it as a friend? When I was in my late teens, I was driven by a desire for three goals to be achieved. First, I wanted, against all odds, to marry Susan. Second, I wanted to secure a law degree and spend my time in court. Third, I wanted to enjoy the benefits that would accrue from a successful legal practice. I would, at the same time, have tried to tie all these desires to a dutiful approach to Matthew 6:33.

I wept when Susan returned to live in America and so was taken from my reach. I wept when my examination results denied me the place I had on offer at Leicester University to study law. I wept at the graveside of my mother. I wept in frustration after my first couple of opportunities to preach as an assistant at

Charlotte Chapel. Now God, in His immense goodness, granted me Susan as a gift and partner in life and
has given me the unimaginable privilege of serving
Him in the church and has opened doors of opportunity that astound me. But when I think of any realistic
progress that is being made, it is unquestionably
linked not with the successes but with the failures and
disappointments and heartaches.

I also recognize that God has preserved me from
much that others have had to face and from whose
example I desperately want to learn. I still shudder
when I think of Jim Elliott's diary and then his brief
life. I am staggered by the commitment of Helen Rose-
veare recorded in *Give Me This Mountain*. I am humbled
by the selfless endeavors of missionaries all over the
world who are paying the price in the cause of the
Gospel. Surely we want to learn to be able to say with
one of the Puritans:

> I am mended by my sickness, enriched by my poverty and
> strengthened by my weakness. . . . What fools are we,
> then, to frown upon our afflictions! These, how crabbed
> soever, are our best friends. They are not indeed for our
> pleasure, they are for our profit.6

CHAPTER SEVEN

The Narrow Way: Never Did a Heedless Person Lead a Holy Life

*I*n John Bunyan's *The Pilgrim's Progress*, there comes a point where Pilgrim encounters two men who have not entered at the gate but have "come tumbling over the wall, on the Left Hand of the narrow Way." Their names are Formalist and Hypocrisy. The dialogue that follows between the two of them and Christian is instructive. Christian asks them why it is that they have chosen not to enter in at the Gate. They respond by saying that it was too much trouble and the short-cut was easier; besides, it has been customary for people to do this for a thousand years.

Turning the tables upon Christian, they challenge him, "Thou art but in the Way, who, as we perceive, came in at the Gate; and we are also in the Way, that came tumbling over the wall: Wherein now is thy condition better than ours?" Christian points out that they are working on the basis of their feelings, whereas he is trusting in the words of his Master, and so he declares,

"You come in by yourselves without his Direction; and shall go out by yourselves without his Mercy."

The biblical foundation for all of this is the statement of Jesus, "I am the gate; whoever enters through me will be saved" (John 10:9). This succinct statement affirms the Christian claim that God has spoken, uniquely, savingly, and finally in Jesus (Hebrews 1:1–2). The writer to the Hebrews drives this home, "But now He has appeared *once for all* at the end of the ages to do away with sin by the sacrifice of himself" (Hebrews 9:26, italics added). In the Sermon on the Mount Jesus says, "Enter through the narrow gate. For wide is the gate and broad is the road that leads to destruction, and many enter through it. But small is the road that leads to life, and only a few find it" (Matthew 7:13–14).

In affirming this, we must immediately recognize that the exclusive nature of these claims flies in the face of our pluralistic society. We are not simply a society in which we recognize the existence of, and differences between, a variety of religious beliefs, but one in which we declare all such beliefs to be equally valid. From that perspective there is only one kind of heresy, namely, to claim that one view is ultimately right, where others are wrong. In granting plausibility to everything, we may grant certainty to nothing. Toleration has been embraced at the expense of truth.

Peter Cotterell points out the destination to which such thinking leads: "If all roads lead to heaven like they do to Timbuctu, then maybe all roads lead to nowhere and for all that I can tell, maybe no road leads to heaven, perhaps all roads lead to hell!" To allow that everyone and everything is right is to destroy the notion of truth itself.

This challenge is not unique to our time. The Israelites were clearly aware that their affirmations of faith were not shared by their neighbors. Christianity operates in the mist of a similar unbelief. Alister McGrath observes: "Christianity was born amidst religious pluralism, and the Christian proclamation has always taken place in a pluralist world, in competition with rival religious and intellectual convictions."[1]

If we are to be able to engage in meaningful conversation with our unbelieving friends, we should understand what they are saying and be prepared to respond. McGrath helps by pointing out that just because people have different religious views, it does not follow that all religious views are equally valid. Furthermore, just because someone is very sincere in his conviction does not mean that it is true. It is possible to be sincerely wrong.

Also, the idea that there are really no substantive differences between religions needs to be held up to careful scrutiny and declared fraudulent. For example, Islam says that Jesus was not crucified. Christianity says He was. Only one of us can be right. Judaism says Jesus was not the Messiah. Christianity says He was. Only one of us can be right. Hinduism says God has often been incarnate. Christianity says God was incarnate only in Jesus. We cannot both be right. Buddhism says that the world's miseries will end when we do what is right. Christianity says we cannot do what is right. The world's miseries will end when we believe what is right.

Christians are often exhorted by detractors to give up our exclusive claims and be "humble" enough to admit the validity of all the other roads. To which we must reply, "Truth is not ultimately a matter of pride or humility; it is a matter of fact." We need then to address the fact of the Incarnation, asking the question, "Who is Jesus and why did He come?" We need also to address the fact of the Resurrection, dealing with "evidence that demands a verdict," as Josh McDowell puts it. All of this is beyond the scope of this chapter, but we recognize in passing that for us to declare the existence of "the narrow way" is to face the challenge of defending our faith without offending our friends.

In *The Pilgrim's Progress*, Formalist and Hypocrisy were pretty sure that entry to the narrow way had to do with observing the law, and they felt confident that in this respect they had as good a record as Christian. The only difference between themselves and him was the coat which he wore. Christian informs them that the coat was given to him by the Lord of Heaven on the day that "He stripped me of my rags." This is a picture of the "righteousness from God" that "comes through faith in Jesus Christ to all who believe" (Romans 3:22).

NOT HEEDLESS

Now that we are on the narrow road, it is essential that we are not heedless. We must not allow some kind of dreamy carelessness to erode our desire to live a holy life. We need to stay awake and alert. We mustn't doze off; we need to pay attention. Solomon constantly urges this upon his readers: "Pay attention and listen to the sayings of the wise; apply your heart to what I teach" (Proverbs 22:17). Anything less than constant vigilance will prove dangerous.

When I was in my late teens, I used to hitch rides to places when I was minus the train fare necessary for the journey I wanted to take. I was often heading north from my home in England to visit friends and relatives in Glasgow, a journey of some two hundred miles. I have made that journey in trucks and vans and cars of various makes and vintage. One particular journey stands out in my recollection. I was hitching on the A1, which for a considerable part of the journey is (or was then) a four-lane road with a median strip and roundabouts every few miles. After I had waited for a while, a gentleman stopped and offered me a ride. His station wagon was in good repair, and in the back he had fishing rods and rifles and two King Charles spaniels. It turned out that he was a farmer from Kent, heading to Scotland for some hunting and fishing. He was finely dressed in plus fours, which is the correct terminology for the apparel unfortunately referred to as knickers by my American cousins.

I was immediately impressed by the speed with which he drove. His approach was to move into high gear as fast as possible and then to stay there as long as possible! There was no question that he was a little erratic, but at eighteen that was a plus. When it happened the first time, it was a little unnerving. At a speed of between seventy and eighty miles per hour, he ran two of the wheels over the narrow curb and onto the central grassy area. He quickly pulled the car back and mumbled an apology. Then I began to watch him carefully out of the corner of my eye. I realized that either he had very heavy eyelids, or he was beginning to doze off at the wheel. When he tried to negotiate a roundabout without gearing down and managed once again to bump the wheels off the curb, I knew it was the latter.

He pulled in for gas and, as he put it, "to stretch his legs," and I seized my chance. As politely as I could, I pointed out that he had already driven a couple of hundred miles from Kent (which, of course, he knew) and that it was obvious to me that he was sleepy. "Oh, I am all right," he replied. That is when I decided on the direct approach. "Sir," I said. "You have already dozed off twice since I've been with you, and if you continue as you are, you might kill yourself and/or someone else. However, it won't be me. Because I cannot drive beside you and feel safe." So I offered to become his chauffeur and drive him to Scotland. He tossed me the keys, got into the passenger seat, and within a short distance fell asleep as we sped toward Scotland. The problem we had faced was not that we were on the wrong road, but that we were endangered on account of his inability to pay attention.

SELF-CONTROLLED

Heedlessness and safety do not go together any more than heedlessness and holy living. On account of this, Peter urges his readers to "be self-controlled and vigilant always, for your enemy the devil is always about, prowling like a lion roaring for its prey" (1 Peter 5:8 PHILLIPS). One of the Puritan writers said of this, "The moment slothfulness begins, that moment dangers stand thick about us." This is in keeping with what many of us were told by our parents, "The devil finds work for idle hands."

Alan Redpath used to talk to young people about the vital importance of what he called "blanket victory." He was referring, not to some strategy for overall success, but to the necessity of getting out of bed at a reasonable time in the morning to pursue the business of the day. If a young person could not get victory over his blankets, it was unlikely that he would be self-controlled in many other areas. It must have cost Peter something to write these words when, after all, it was in this very area that he had proved a failure. Jesus had told him, along with the others, to "Watch and pray." Peter had done neither, and despite all his high-sounding affirmations of allegiance to Jesus he had capitulated when questioned by a servant girl.

THE MIND PREPARED FOR ACTION

Is it any wonder that in seeking to strengthen the brethren as Jesus had told him, Peter should emphasize this most vital area? In his first letter, when he has introduced the nature of salvation, he moves to application, and first on his list is a call to holy living. "Therefore, prepare your minds for action; be self-controlled" (1 Peter 1:13). In the King James Version the phrase reads, "gird up the loins of your mind." The word *gird* refers to the habit of quickly gathering up the loose robes of the Middle East with a belt when in a hurry or starting on a journey. This is because the long flowing robes would impede physical activity unless tucked under the belt. Similarly, we need to be alert and prepared, both mentally and spiritually.

I always tell young people that if they are going to be effective in dealing with temptation, then they must recognize the battle for their minds. Temptation of all kinds is a reality, and in our sex-crazed culture there is perhaps no greater challenge than to live in purity before marriage and fidelity after marriage.

The Old Testament provides us with two particularly telling illustrations in this area. We can learn from both: in the first case, what we shouldn't do; and in the second, what we should.

David became king when he was thirty years old. He conquered Jerusalem and was established in his palace. He defeated the Philistines, brought the ark to Jerusalem, and, as he ruled over all Israel, he did what was just and right for all his people. He declared his sensitive compassion in his generous care of Mephibosheth, the crippled son of his best friend. With matters of state well under control and surrounded by the benefits of his God-given success, he might have appeared invincible. Yet, whether or not David recognized it, he was very vulnerable to temptation.

One evening he got up from his bed and took a stroll on the roof of his palace. From that vantage point he saw a woman bathing—and, we are told, she was very beautiful. Now, at that point he had a decision to make. As I work on this computer, it constantly asks me whether I want to "create a file" or "save" or "close" or "exit." My response to one question has a direct implication for all that follows. In David's case, he should have hit the "exit" key, and he should have hit it fast. Instead, he determined in that moment that he would "create a file." What should he name it? Well, he sent a man to find out about her. It turned out that this very beautiful lady was Bathsheba, the wife of Uriah the Hittite, one of his generals.

When that information reached him, David had a second decision to make, and once again he chose badly. He sent his messengers to get Bathsheba, and the sorry saga of adultery and murder that followed can all be traced to his unwillingness to nip temptation in the bud. He had no one to blame but himself. James describes the way in which the process unfolds: "Each one is tempted when, by his own evil desire, he is dragged away and enticed. Then, after desire has conceived, it gives birth to sin; and sin, when it is full-grown, gives birth to death" (James 1:14–15).

As a boy, I learned from a number of sources the following verse, which is worthy of memorization:

> Sow a thought, reap an action.
> Sow an action, reap a habit.
> Sow a habit, reap a character.
> Sow a character, reap a destiny.

And then my teachers would often add the words of Paul to the Galatians, "Be not deceived; God is not mocked: for whatsoever a man soweth, that shall he also reap" (Galatians 6:7 KJV).

FIGHTING TEMPTATIONS

There is never a time (until heaven) when we are exempt from temptation. Recognizing this ought to help us prepare for the battle. God's word to Cain has a chilling relevance for all of us: "Sin is crouching at your door; it desires to have you, but you must master it" (Genesis 4:7).

In direct contrast to David's failure, we have the record of Joseph. In modern psycho-babble he would be described as having come from a dysfunctional family. Adored and spoiled by his father and hated by his brothers, he was dumped at the side of the road and ended up in Egypt. God was overruling all these circumstances, and Joseph ended up in a position of key responsibility in the home of Potiphar, one of the Pharaoh's officials. Joseph was completely trusted by his master, who had delegated everything to his care.

His master's wife became infatuated with him because he was well built and handsome. She tried to seduce him and was not particularly subtle in her approach. Joseph declared himself to be a man of principle as he refused her advances. He pointed out that such wickedness would not only violate his master's trust, but it would also be to "sin against God." But she did not give up. On a daily basis she sought to entice him, but he consistently refused. He was wise enough to make sure that he wasn't even in her company, never mind her bed. So persistent was she in her advances that he eventually eluded her grasp by running off down the street.

So Joseph ends up in jail rather than in bed! He is a perfect example of the very opposite of heedlessness. He was paying attention. He was self-controlled and alert. He was operating on the basis of principle and not on the platform of fluctuating feelings. He could just as easily have allowed himself to become infatuated by Potiphar's wife. But he didn't.

Over the years I have had too many occasions when I have had to sit and listen to a man tell me that he has never "felt" this way about a woman before, the inference being that his feelings somehow legitimized his sinful behavior. Such a man has failed to learn the importance of appointing moral sentries at the vulnerable places of his mind. He will often talk about how he is asking God to "take away" these feelings, but he is unprepared to be like Joseph and alter his calendar and his location to ensure that he is not leading himself into temptation. We need to help one another to apply the Scriptures in these most vital of areas. "Look upon yourselves as dead to the appeal and power of sin but alive and sensitive to the call of God" (Romans 6:11 Phillips).

David was heedless and Joseph was alert. How are we to deal with temptation so as to avoid the failure of David and follow Joseph's example? Three words provide a useful answer:

1. *Immediately*. The time to deal with temptations is in their beginnings. Whenever you see the first signs of rust on your car, it is a good idea to have it treated. Failure to do so will only lead to bigger problems later. It is far easier to redirect the course of a tiny stream than it is to try to dam up a large and fast-flowing river. If we are watching a film that prevents us from thinking about whatever is pure and holy and of good report, we should switch it off or walk away—immediately. There is no good reason to allow the unhelpful images to take hold of our minds.

2. *Ruthlessly*. This is what Jesus meant when He said, "If your right eye causes you to sin, gouge it out and throw it away. It is better for you to lose one part

of your body than for your whole body to be thrown into hell" (Matthew 5:29). He then says the same thing about "your right hand." Church leaders today tiptoe around sin, fearful of offending or troubling those who are involved. Jesus was straight and to the point, and His advice is clear to understand and crucial in its application. Paul speaks about beating his body and making it his slave, so as to ensure that when he has preached to others, he will not be disqualified from the prize. Can we do less?

3. *Consistently.* Joseph's ability to say no is striking in the first instance. But when we read that he was subjected to the seductive ploys of the woman on a daily basis and still he said no, we are awestruck by the enabling power of God and Joseph's mastery of himself. I have in the past had a particular problem with Planter's peanuts. I like them too much. I have enlisted the help of my wife to keep them away from me, and myself from them. We are not good together! Sometimes when I go somewhere and they are offered to me, I resist them immediately, and I have been known to banish them ruthlessly from my presence. But, if they keep coming around, and I am offered them continually, my early victories only serve to make my final defeat all the more crushing. That is a very minor illustration of what in other matters may prove to be a major problem.

I tell young couples on their wedding day that if they are to be true to their vows, it will be important for them to determine immediately that they will only have eyes for each other. They must refuse to allow their eyes to wander, their minds to contemplate, and their affections to run after anyone who would draw them away from each other. The same is true in our relationship with Jesus. When we become conscious of sinful thoughts, suggestions, desires, and longings, we must learn to say no on a consistent basis.

As we "work out [our] salvation with fear and trembling," we must remember that "it is God who works in you to will and to act according to his good purpose" (Philippians 2:12–13). The paraphrase given in *The Living Bible* is particularly clear: "For God is at work within you, helping you want to obey him, and then helping you do what he wants." Paul tells the Romans, "For those God foreknew he also predestined to be conformed to the likeness of his Son" (Romans 8:29).

This is part of the explanation of discipline in the believer's life. "God disciplines us for our good, that we may share in his holiness" (Hebrews 12:10). William Gurnall writes, "God would not rub so hard if it were not to fetch out the dirt that is ingrained in our natures. God loves purity so well He had rather see a hole than a spot in His child's garments."[2] Even in our failures and disappointments, in our wanderings and shortcomings, God is at work to bring to completion in our lives the work which His goodness began.

CHAPTER EIGHT

Intellectualism and Materialism: Chasing After the Wind

Everyone would agree that seeking protection from a bullet by holding up sheets of paper is nothing short of foolishness. It is an experiment to be conducted only once. However, not everyone would agree that attempting to shield ourselves from bleakness and emptiness by stocking up on "earthly produce" is equally futile. We succumb to the allure of modern advertising and are captivated by the outward show of things without inquiring into their real value, in the hope that acquiring new things will remove our sense of dissatisfaction.

The psalmist declares his dependence to be upon the Lord at all times and for all things. "My help comes from the Lord, the maker of heaven and earth" (Psalm 121:2). Whenever we place our trust in anyone or anything other than God, it is sin. Alister McGrath has stated: "Sin moves us away from God, and tempts us to place other things in his place. Created things thus come to be substituted for God. And they do not satisfy."[1]

When the Beatles hit center stage in the early sixties, they were very honest about their expectations. They sang about wanting money because, like so many others, they apparently saw it as the universal key to contentment. Within a relatively short period they had recognized that money can't buy love and that the latter was the more significant of the two. If possessions and fame, by themselves, could relieve our troubled minds, then those who had most of each would presumably be the happiest. But we know that this is not the case.

Jesus warned His listeners in the Sermon on the Mount about investing in the wrong securities: "Do not store up for yourselves treasures on earth, where moth and rust destroy, and where thieves break in and steal" (Matthew 6:19). We should not succumb to the temptation to live as though our security is here. Our ultimate investment strategy should focus our attention on heaven. "But store up for yourselves treasures in heaven, where moth and rust do not destroy, and where thieves do not break in and steal" (Matthew 6:20). For the fact of the matter is that our hearts will follow our profits.

Are we then to adopt an entirely negative attitude toward things? Of all the good gifts which God has given us to enjoy, the two that bring the greatest human benefit—and, when misused, the greatest human evil—are sex and wealth. The response of medieval sainthood toward sex and money was to embrace celibacy and poverty. Such a radical and ruthless response has an appearance of wisdom, but man-made rules are incapable of conquering evil thoughts and restraining sensual indulgence. We need instead to follow Moses, who called the people of his day to "remember the Lord your God, for it is he who gives you the ability to produce wealth" (Deuteronomy 8:18).

Paul gave Timothy clear instructions concerning those who have done well financially and materially. They should not be arrogant or put their confidence in their wealth. Instead they should be encouraged to "put their hope in God, who richly provides us with everything for our enjoyment" (1 Timothy 6:17). They should hold material goods and wealth on a flat palm and not in a clenched fist.

INTELLECTUAL AVENUE: INTELLECTUALISM

The writer of Ecclesiastes became a devoted student of and gave himself to the pursuit of wisdom. However, he was quick to conclude, "With much wisdom comes much sorrow; the more knowledge, the more grief" (Ecclesiastes 1:18). Einstein is reputed to have exclaimed, "I have discovered that the men who know the most are the most gloomy." The pursuit of knowledge is worthwhile, and our minds matter. Our faith is historic and capable of rigorous investigation.

We would want to distance ourselves from mindless religion. But the jigsaw puzzle of life cannot be successfully assembled by intellect alone.

I am told that in the past the high tower of Durham Cathedral has been closed during final exams at the university. This was done to prevent further suicide attempts. Those who had already taken that sorry route were not the dropouts and the marginal students; they were those from the first-class honors category. They were bright enough to understand that their anticipated academic success would be insufficient to fill the void in their lives. But their intellectual diet contained too much of this kind of material from the fourth century: "None of us knows anything, not even when we know or do not know, nor do we know whether knowing or not knowing exist, nor in general where there is anything or not." This from the pen of Metrodorus of Chios, a fourth-century Greek philosopher.

Such earthly wisdom is insufficient to satisfy the longing for meaning. Equally empty are Jean Paul Sartre's words: "Every existent is born without reason, prolongs itself out of weakness and dies by chance." Such ideas are capable of creating trouble of spirit but certainly not of curing it.

Malcolm Muggeridge, in his book *Jesus Rediscovered*, says that "education, the great mumbo-jumbo and fraud of the ages, purports to equip us to live, and is prescribed as a universal remedy for everything from juvenile delinquency to premature senility, [but] for the most part . . . only serves to enlarge stupidity, inflate conceit and put those subjected to it at the mercy of brainwashers with printing presses, radio and T.V. at their disposal."[2]

FOOLISH STREET: CYNICISM

The writer of Ecclesiastes talks about embracing madness and folly. There is more to this than at first appears. When the Bible speaks of fools and folly, it is referring not to mental deficiency but moral perversity. The essence of such folly is summarized in the psalmist's words: "The fool says in his heart, 'There is no God'" (Psalm 14:1). First, we deny God's existence, and then we deny life's values. The words of Dostoyevsky express it well: "If God is dead, then everything is permitted." Paul explains this in the opening chapter of Romans. What may be known about God is plain. But man suppresses the truth, and although he knows he does so, he refuses to admit it and lives with the consequences.

The paraphrase of the passage given in *The Living Bible* captures vividly the way the rejection of the truth works itself out: "After awhile they began to think up silly ideas of what God was like and what he wanted them to do. The result was that their foolish minds became dark and confused. Claiming themselves to be wise without God, they became utter fools instead" (Romans 1:21–22 TLB). This confusion and foolishness can be seen in the lack of order that marks so much

modern art, the baseness of much contemporary literature, and the emptiness of a great deal that passes for
humor.

In the early 1970s Monty Python's *Flying Circus*
was responsible for pushing the parameters of humor
well beyond the boundaries of what was then acceptable. However, it quickly became cynical and destruc-
tive as it embraced the obscene, the absurd, and the
irrational. When we learn to laugh at everything,
nothing is worth the bother of a laugh. Some who
have spent their lives making others laugh have
proved to be figures of despair. Peter Sellers, of *Pink
Panther* fame, was reportedly unhappy, and one of his
biographies caught the emptiness of his life in the title
The Mask Behind the Mask. I recall seeing one of his
friends interviewed after Sellers had died. His friend,
who admired him, said that Peter Sellers had been in
many ways an empty figure who only came alive when
given a part to play. His personal life was, in dramatic
terms, a tragedy, and so he yearned to be the clowns
he played.

In Great Britain in the 1960s there was a famous
comedian named Tony Hancock. His weekly televi-
sion program was watched by millions who admired
his sardonic wit. His last TV monologue in 1964
proved an ironic farewell. The best you can expect of
life, he said, "is a few daffodils in a jam jar, a rough
hewn stone bearing the legend 'He came and he went'
and in between—nothing! Nobody will even notice

you're not here. . . . Nobody will ever know I existed. Nothing to leave behind me. . . . Nobody to mourn me. That's the bitterest blow of all."[3]

Hancock spent the final months of his life as a sorry recluse, refusing mostly to get out of bed. He would pull the covers over his head, unable to face life and unaided by his humorous abilities. He died alone of an overdose in 1968.

Despite the fact that such stories are all too common, Intellectual Avenue and Foolish Street remain crowded with travelers who are tempted to believe that they will find on these thoroughfares the satisfaction for which they long.

PLEASURE PARKWAY: HEDONISM

Here we find the writer of Ecclesiastes creating a world for himself where he made the rules and then broke them as required. He worked hard for what he had. His homes and parks and lakes were well cared for by his large staff. Had he lived today, his face would appear regularly on the cover of *People* magazine. His life was filled with wine and women and entertainment. He had tickets for all the best shows, the best seats in the house, and the right kind of company. If prestige were the key to life, he held it in his hand. But it wasn't and he didn't. Each key proved only to open another door to disillusionment. He knew the bitter truth expressed in the poetry of Robert Burns:

But pleasures are like poppies spread—
You seize the flow'r, its bloom is shed;
Or like the snow falls in the river—
A moment white—then melts forever.[4]

FAST TRACK VALLEY: MATERIALISM

"All his days his work is pain and grief; even at night his mind does not rest" (Ecclesiastes 2:23).

For a while our church offices were in a building we shared with realtors, bankers, doctors, and lawyers. One morning as I arrived early, I met one of the attorneys in the hallway. "You look like you've been here a while," I said. His reply was classic. "Yes. I awoke at 3:30 A.M. and could not sleep, so I came to work!" It would be one thing if he enjoyed a sense of deep satisfaction from all his toil, but by his own testimony he was trapped in the endless cycle: working to get money to buy food to stay alive to go to work to get money to buy food to stay alive.

The description of a man all alone, a workaholic and yet not content with what he has achieved, fits the condition of many people. He had provided everything for his children that money could buy but failed to give them what they wanted most—his time, attention, and affection. To whom will he leave it when he goes?

I was being treated to a round of golf by one of my neighbors. We were eating lunch in his club prior to playing. Two of his work colleagues made up the four-some. So there we were. Three stockbrokers and a pastor. They were each managing significant sums of money for wealthy clients. In the course of conversation I asked, "How many of your clients would you say are contented?" They asked me to repeat the question and then sat in silence.

Eventually, as they went around the table, they concluded that between them they could not think of one! We then went on to discuss the immediate relevance of the words of the apostle Paul: "Godliness with contentment is great gain" (1 Timothy 6:6). The men were unaware of the source of the statement, and once identified, it opened up a significant discussion that underlined their awareness that possession of all kinds of material things cannot be said to produce contentment or compensate for a troubled soul. In his first letter to Timothy, Paul says of material things:

1. We arrived with nothing and we will leave with nothing.
2. We can be content with the basics of food and clothing.
3. People who constantly think about getting rich face severe temptations and dangerous traps.
4. The love of money is a root of all kinds of evil.
5. Some money-grabbing people have wandered from faith and live in grief.

How is it possible to tell whether we are guilty of an inordinate love of money? A friend of mine has identified a number of tell-tale signs that are a distinct challenge. I am guilty of loving money when:

1. Thoughts of money consume my day.
2. Others' success makes me jealous.
3. I define success in terms of what I have rather than what I am in Christ.
4. My family is neglected in my pursuit of money.
5. I close my eyes to the genuine needs of others.
6. I am living in the paralyzing fear of losing it.
7. I am prepared to borrow myself into bondage.
8. God gets my leftovers, rather than my first fruits.

The book *Three Men in a Boat*, by Jerome K. Jerome,[5] tells the story of three friends who take a boat trip down the river Thames. Before setting out on their voyage, they list what they regard as indispensable cargo. When they realize that the river will not allow for the navigation of a boat sufficiently large to take the things they regard as indispensable, they tear up the list. At that point, one of the three has a moment of insight.

"You know we are on the wrong track altogether. We must not think of the things we could do with, but only of the things we can't do without." One of the others comments on the "downright wisdom" of such an approach and proceeds to apply the principle to the trip up the river of life. "How many people, on that voyage, load up the boat till it is in danger of swamping with a store of foolish things which they think essential to the pleasure and comfort of the trip." He then describes the possessions that are "useless lumber" and should be thrown overboard. Failure to do so will result in never knowing a moment's freedom from anxiety and care and the loss of the chance to "smell the roses" and enjoy the beauties of nature. So he urges:

> Let your boat of life be light, packed with only what you need—a homely home and simple pleasures, one or two friends, worth the name, someone to love and someone to love you. . . . You will find the boat easier to pull then and it will not be so liable to upset, and it will not matter so much if it does upset; good, plain merchandise will stand water. You will have time to think as well as to work.6

That kind of thinking is in accord with Paul's statement "If we have food and clothing, we will be content with that" (1 Timothy 6:8), and it is a metaphor of the way we should live our lives.

CHAPTER NINE

*Putting On
the Garment
of Humility*

$\mathcal{T}$his is the one I esteem: he who is humble and contrite in spirit, and trembles at my word" (Isaiah 66:2).

Humility pleases God. But humility is not in fashion. It would be sad if we had simply forgotten about it, allowed it to fade from view with the passing of time. But the evidence suggests that it is not that we have merely allowed it to slip; we have voted it out of the public domain. We appear to have concluded that just as smoking is hazardous and should be restricted, so too should humility.

On a number of occasions in the late 1980s I was given the opportunity to speak to public school teachers during their in-service training days. These events proved to be fascinating and enjoyable engagements and gave me entry to a world I had only seen from the other side of the desk.

My brief on these occasions was straightforward—to be inspirational—and I believe I accomplished that objective. But eventually the invitations dried up. I think that may have been because I based my remarks, on one occasion, on the words of Jeremiah 9:23–24: "This is what the Lord says: 'Let not the wise man boast of his wisdom or the strong man boast of his strength or the rich man boast of his riches, but let him who boasts boast about this: that he understands and knows me, that I am the Lord.'"

I suggested that our culture's preoccupation with brains, bodies, and bucks needed to be reexamined in light of the product emerging from our homes and schools. I was always interested to see their program for the day and to note the areas of emphasis in child development and teaching strategy. On each occasion I searched in vain for any hint that humility might be considered as a necessary prerequisite for effective education. Rather, the drift seemed to be to encourage children to write papers on such subjects as "Why I am important," or, "Why I love myself." Far from encouraging the children to see humility as a positive attribute to be cultivated, too often it was depicted as a liability to be avoided. In contrast, the Scripture says, "This is the one I esteem: he who is humble and contrite in spirit, and trembles at my word" (Isaiah 66:2).

An earlier generation might have overemphasized the maxim "Children are to be seen and not heard." (Correctly applied, this maxim does not prescribe silence always and everywhere.) The pendulum has now swung to the opposite extreme, whereby children are always to be seen and heard. Lest as parents we should be tempted to correct the balance, we are provided with bumper stickers for our minivans, allowing us to drive around our neighborhoods boasting about our children.

This absence of humility is so pervasive we are liable to miss it unless someone points it out. A sign on a college student's door satirized the attitude. In bold print it read: "NO, I AM NOT CONCEITED," then underneath, in smaller type, "Though I have every right to be so."

Olympic athletes interviewed following their medal ceremonies unashamedly declare: "I am very proud of myself and of what I have done." No longer do we hear a modest response: "It has been an immense privilege to represent my country. I am deeply grateful to those who selflessly helped to train me, and I am humbled by this success."

We have grown up in a generation that has taken as its anthem a song frequently sung by Frank Sinatra, "My Way." Yet what is the result of "My Way" in the singer's life? Today's newspaper carries the account of the singer, now aged seventy-eight, collapsing on stage during the performance of that song. The article describes how he was removed in a wheelchair. His experience illustrates Isaiah's words: "All men are like grass, and all their glory is like the flowers of the field. The grass withers and the flowers fall, because the breath of the Lord blows on them" (Isaiah 40:6–7).

In search of classic illustrations of humility, I turned to the compendium of epigrams and stories compiled by William J. Bennett, *The Book of Virtues*. I fully expected to find a complete section devoted to humility alongside such listings as honesty and loyalty, but it wasn't there. Now I imagine that the explanation could be that the presence of humility is implied throughout the book, and certainly the stories depict it. But that isn't enough. The virtue of humility needs to be acknowledged directly.

If we instill the characteristics of work, courage, and perseverance in our children but do not instill in them the grace of humility, they will be marked by the spirit of the Pharisee: virtuous in many ways but too proud to see their need of God. King Uzziah had perseverance and loyalty, but his empire and influence crumbled because of a lack of humility. "After Uzziah became powerful, his pride led to his downfall" (2 Chronicles 26:16).

THE LIFE OF NEBUCHADNEZZAR

The Bible is full of warnings about the devastating effect of pride. There is no more dramatic case study on this subject in the Old Testament than that of the fall and rise of the Babylonian king, Nebuchadnezzar.

We are introduced to this king in the early chapters of Daniel. He would have been a hard one to have on your Christmas list. What do you buy for the man who has everything? He was living in his "golden years," enjoying security on his borders and prosperity in his land. All the economic indicators were strong. Had he lived today, his public pronouncements would have been covered by national and international networks. The success of his military policy matched the grandeur of his palace and gardens. He was in control, the master of all he surveyed. His problem certainly wasn't low self-esteem.

Jesus spoke of another whose pride in his accomplishments spelled imminent danger. That person had built bigger barns to house his crops and looked forward to a life of pleasure and indulgence. "But God said to him, 'You fool! This very night your life will be demanded from you. Then who will get what you have prepared for yourself?'" (Luke 12:20).

So it was with Nebuchadnezzar. He had a palace, power, and prosperity, but, in the goodness of God, he was to discover that he also had a problem. He is awakened in the night by a dark, disturbing dream. In his terror, he calls for his wizards, who are unable to guess as to the interpretation. Then Daniel is called to listen to the details of the dream and to interpret them.

When Daniel realizes what he is dealing with, he is perplexed and alarmed. Nebuchadnezzar had been shaken because he did not understand the meaning of the dream, but Daniel is dismayed because he understands it perfectly. He confronts the king with tact and wisdom. "My Lord, if only the dream applied to your enemies and its meaning to your adversaries!" (Daniel

4:19). Then he declared the message: "You, O king, are that tree" (4:22).

Daniel identifies the king's underlying problem as pride. Up to this point Nebuchadnezzar has failed to acknowledge that heaven rules. His world was bound north, south, east, and west by himself. That must change. His is not a problem with low self-esteem. It is an illustration of sin, aptly described by William Temple: "I make myself, in a host of ways, the center of the universe."

There is no "nondirective" counseling here! No suggestion from Daniel that the king's problem lies in his being a victim of his background or circumstances. Nor does Daniel beat around the bush or talk in vague generalities. He keeps nothing back.

Men and women need to be made aware of the critical position they are in before Almighty God. This is as true in private counseling as it is in public proclamation. It is easy to capitulate to the desire for public affirmation. Almost imperceptibly and usually over a period of time, the preacher slides into vague generalities that neither offend nor carry with them the possibility of lasting change. In a generation of wafflers and storytellers and pseudo-psychological gurus, the question surely remains: Where are the prophetic voices that, like Nathan, are prepared to say to the king, "You are the man"?

What was Nebuchadnezzar to do if he was to have a possibility of reprieve? "Acknowledge that the Most

High is sovereign over the kingdoms of men," Daniel told him (4:25). Nebuchadnezzar must look away from himself and fix his gaze upon God and His glory. But the king displayed contempt for the riches of God's kindness, tolerance, and patience. Judgment struck. "He was driven away from people and ate grass like cattle. His body was drenched with the dew of heaven until his hair grew like the feathers of an eagle and his nails like the claws of a bird" (4:33).

Can you imagine the amazement of the palace servants as he who had been couched in splendor is no longer allowed on the couch; as he who once looked down on all he surveyed now gazes on his palace from a pasture, where he munches grass? Can he be restored to sanity, and what are the steps back?

"I RAISED MY EYES TOWARD HEAVEN"

Up to this point Nebuchadnezzar had never looked beyond the ramparts and balustrades of his own architectural genius. Now, driven from his palace by insanity, he gains a new perspective: "I raised my eyes toward heaven." In this "look" he is like the young man in the story told by Jesus in Luke 15, who also "came to his senses."

"MY SANITY WAS RESTORED"

When Nebuchadnezzar thinks seriously about God and His glory, he is able to come to terms with himself and his need. Calvin says, "Man never achieves a clear knowledge of himself unless he has first looked upon God's face, and then descends from contemplating Him to scrutinize himself," and that is true of Nebuchadnezzar. God had been remote for Nebuchadnezzar, but now He is a personal God to whom he owes honor. In that moment, the king's sanity is restored.

"THEN I PRAISED THE MOST HIGH"

Pride gives way to praise. He had believed himself to be on the pinnacle of success, but God has shown him that he was really in a slimy pit. Nebuchadnezzar cried to the Lord, and was lifted out and set on a rock and given a new song, a hymn of praise to God. "My Way" was been replaced with "His Way."

> His dominion is an eternal dominion; his kingdom endures from generation to generation. All the peoples of the earth are regarded as nothing. He does as he pleases with the powers of heaven and the peoples of the earth. No one can hold back his hand or say to him: "What have you done?" (Daniel 4:34–35)

Only God Himself can effect such a change in the heart of the proud.

PRIDE STILL REIGNS TODAY

We may be tempted to believe that Nebuchadnezzar's story is historically interesting but practically irrelevant. Only pride prevents us from facing our absence of personal humility.

Most of us have little empires—professional, academic, commercial, ecclesiastical realms in which we believe ourselves to be more significant than we are. It is easy for us to talk about what we have accomplished rather than what God in His goodness has chosen to bless. We use much that happens around us to feed our egos rather than fuel our humility. We must fight this monster ruthlessly. One of my friends says, speaking tongue-in-cheek but with no small truth, "It is important for a pastor to have a wife, if for no other reason than to keep him humble." So it is with persons in all professions.

What about our culture's preoccupation with personality? Many local churches have more of this problem than we would care to admit. We dare not use our spiritual gifts as a source of self-aggrandizement. And what of the increasingly commonplace emphasis on self-esteem as the key to effective Christian living? Again, we should not be unsympathetic to those whose lives have been crippled by a negative view of self, but always, and in every case, psychological theory must bow the knee to biblical theology.

THE POWER OF THE WORD OF GOD

Here we return to humility. We must learn what it means to tremble at God's Word. When Peter concluded his sermon on the day of Pentecost, the people "were cut to the heart" and inquired about what they should do (Acts 2:37). When Paul preached to Felix and Drusilla in Acts 24, Felix trembled. But there is little likelihood of such a response when we settle for delivering or listening to amiable chats and sentimental stories that tickle our ears but do not touch our souls.

We need biblical exposition that drives the truth home. Humility means recognizing and believing that "unless the Lord builds the house, its builders labor in vain" (Psalm 127:1). It means acknowledging that apart from Jesus we can do nothing as we ought. It means longing to be filled with God's Word and God's Spirit.

THE WORD OF GOD DWELLING RICHLY IN US

In Colossians 3, Paul urges his readers to "let the word of Christ dwell in you richly" (v. 16). We need to listen to the Scriptures being faithfully taught. Every Christian should make it a priority to sit regularly under the careful, practical exposition of the Bible. Such exposition is one of the duties of pastor-teachers, those men given as a gift to the church to "prepare God's people for works of service" (Ephesians 4:12) so that the church may become mature.

I have yet to meet an effective believer who neglected feeding on God's Word. When Ezra preached to the people in Nehemiah 8, the attitude with which the listeners came to hear him was crucial. We need to follow their example by committing ourselves to attend expectantly, listen carefully, and apply the Scriptures properly. Then we can leave the service with joyful hearts.

James is clear about the danger of not seeing ourselves ruthlessly. "Do not merely listen to the word,
and so deceive yourselves. Do what it says" (James
1:22). Cultivate friends or engage the help of your
spouse to give you an honest evaluation of how you
are doing in applying the Word to your life.

We should not rely on only one good meal or two a
week. Many of us are neglectful of the Scriptures on a
daily basis. We have the best of intentions on a Sunday,
but our follow-through is lacking. It is important that
we develop a system of Bible study that takes us
through the whole of Scripture and keeps us faithful in
our reading. Over the years I have used a number of
approaches as a means of keeping on track. Robert
Murray McCheyne's diary of readings is one of them. It
allows me to read through the whole Bible in the space
of a year. A similar approach could be used for the New
Testament alone. Scripture Union notes are valuable, as
are the various devotional booklets, such as *Walk
through the Bible* and *Today in the Word*. The method is not
as important as the discipline it helps to create.

Meditate upon and memorize portions of Scripture. I find it helpful to select from my daily reading a
verse or even a phrase that I can take into my day. Just
the other day, in reading the first chapter of 1 Thessalonians, I was struck by Paul's statement that the
Gospel had come to his readers "not simply with
words, but also with power, with the Holy Spirit and
with deep conviction" (v. 5). In spending "vacant

moments" of the day pondering such passages, I feed my soul, stir my mind, and usually commit to memory another brief passage.

It is also good to attempt more major memorization. One of my colleagues and I began recently to memorize 2 Timothy. I am still only halfway through chapter 2, while Dave has already completed the project.

Pray the Scriptures into the core of your being. Once again, this means something more than mere head knowledge. It involves the assimilation of biblical truth into your very substance. Spurgeon used to talk of becoming the kind of biblical Christians who, if cut, would actually bleed the Bible. Such fullness surely does not come about as a result of simply attending seminars or filling our journals with notes but emerges from time on our knees with our Bibles open before us.

THE HOLY SPIRIT IN OUR LIVES

We are commanded to be filled with the Spirit. The Bible tells us that when we hunger and thirst after righteousness we will be filled (Matthew 5:6). Jesus explained that, if we as earthly fathers knew how to give good gifts to our children, how much more would our heavenly Father give the Holy Spirit to them that ask Him (Matthew 7:11). The apostle John reports:

On the last and greatest day of the Feast [of Tabernacles],

Jesus stood and said in a loud voice, "If anyone is thirsty, let him come to me and drink. Whoever believes in me, as the Scripture has said, streams of living water will flow from within him." By this he meant the Spirit, whom those who believed in him were later to receive. (John 7:37–39)

We need to allow the Holy Spirit to work in our lives. The fullness of God's Spirit is not the unique privilege of a few but the birthright of all who are in Christ. The promise of Jesus in John 14:23 is for all his disciples: "If anyone loves me, he will obey my teaching. My Father will love him, and we will come to him and make our home with him." It is not possible, says Paul, to belong to Christ without having the Spirit of Christ (Romans 8:9).

The evidences of a Spirit-filled life are both gifts and fruit. As someone once said, "The gifts of the Spirit are tools to be used, not toys to be played with." Careful study of passages such as 1 Corinthians 12, Romans 12, and 1 Peter 4 help us to understand this. Galatians 5:22 provides us with a list of the facets that comprise the fruit God produces in our lives—a very attractive picture.

All too often we have sought to circumscribe the ministry of God's Spirit, despite the fact that it is depicted in terms of two of the most uncontrollable aspects of nature—wind and fire. We have settled for adequacy when God's purpose for us is abundance.

Much emphasis is placed upon the fact that the

tense of the verb in Ephesians 5:18 is in the present continuous—keep on being filled. This tense is used in the passage to emphasize that spiritual fullness is not about a crisis but rather about a process. While agreeing with this perspective, I think we have to be honest enough to recognize that when an individual has been through a period of spiritual dryness and comes with a renewed and genuine thirst to drink of God's Spirit, that may then be viewed as something of at least a minor crisis.

This does not mean that believers should live their lives in an ongoing crisis. However, we cannot expect that disobedient and wandering believers, who are living in a form of spiritual famine, may be brought into an experience of God's fullness without recognizing the difference.

Where a life has been singularly used of God, there is no question but that it has had all the marks of spiritual fullness. Whether we embrace the framework of contemporary charismatic circles or do not, we are forced to conclude that all that is accomplished for good in the kingdom is clearly in light of and in line with the truth of Zechariah 4:6: "Not by might nor by power, but by my Spirit, says the Lord Almighty."

RELYING ON CHRIST AND "HIM CRUCIFIED"

When the apostle Paul addressed the citizens of Corinth, he acknowledged his education and spoke as a reasonable man, but he was not afraid to base his address on something that was thought to be foolish: the Gospel message.

Signs and wonders may have been the order of the day, but Paul chose to stay with the proclamation of "Jesus Christ and him crucified" (1 Corinthians 2:2). There was nothing with less popular appeal. He might have pointed out the extent and quality of his educational background, but instead he chose to declare what was regarded by society as foolish, because that was the message God had chosen to honor by the accompanying power of His Spirit. Until we are prepared to be thought foolish in the eyes of the world, it is unlikely that we will know the power of God being displayed in our lives and ministries.

THE FRAGRANT AROMA OF CHRIST

The dramatic impact of the ministry of Peter and John caused the people to take note of them. Luke explains the reason: "When they saw the courage of Peter and John and realized that they were unschooled, ordinary men, they were astonished and they took note that these men had been with Jesus" (Acts 4:13). It is only when we come from the presence of Christ that we may enter the thoroughfares of life with power. This is not something that is intangible, impractical, or even mystical.

One of the simple pleasures of my life is in spending time with my sisters' husbands. It is always possible to tell when I have been driving with Paul because I come home marked by the distinct aroma of his car. The issue is not one of personal hygiene. As a veterinarian, he spends a lot of time with large animals, and his car is pervaded by a mixture of medicinal and agricultural odors, so much so that it is impossible to spend time with him without becoming marked by a certain "fragrance." This is how it is in spending time with Jesus, says the apostle. "Thanks be to God, who always leads us in triumphal procession in Christ and through us spreads everywhere the fragrance of the knowledge of him" (2 Corinthians 2:14).

There is tremendous encouragement in all of this. We must learn to think of ourselves with sober judgment, not more highly than we ought. God is not looking for the powerful and the successful and those who are able communicators. Instead, he looks for the person who has a broken and a contrite spirit. Those individuals, whether they are extroverted or introverted, humorous or melancholy, are regularly in the quiet place bowing before God's Word with a trembling heart and seeking fresh enabling from the Holy Spirit. They have been brought to see that they did not make themselves, nor did they save themselves. They are totally dependent upon God's grace.

THE GARMENT OF HUMILITY

The Bible does not call us to "feel humble" but to adopt an attitude of lowliness. This lowliness is like a garment that reveals itself in servanthood. We should not leave home without it. When the garment of humility is absent, friendships are marred, families are broken, and fellowships are destroyed. An attitude of humility thinks about serving and giving, just as Jesus did when He washed the feet of His disciples. Peter, to whom the absence of humility was not unknown, reminds the readers of his first letter, "Humble yourselves, therefore, under God's mighty hand, that he may lift you up in due time" (1 Peter 5:6).

We do not want to reject the essential place of a good education. Nor do we want to embrace some kind of mystical mindlessness. Instead, we need to apply our minds with diligence, recognizing that we can do nothing as we ought without divine enabling.

It is said that someone once asked Thomas à Kempis how it was that he had been so mightily used by God. He is reputed to have replied, "I can only assume that God looked down from heaven to find the smallest and most insignificant creature and seeing me, He took me up and used me." What a wonder to realize that, despite our inadequacies and failures and our lack of powerful resources, God takes up yet another old clay pot, to show that the power belongs to Him alone.

CHAPTER TEN

Evangelism: The Necessity of Bringing Others to Christ

If I want to be approved at the last, nothing can take the place of my making an honest, sincere, and prayerful effort to bring others to the Savior. Our situation is similar to that of four lepers sitting at the city gates of Samaria during a siege in the time of the prophet Elisha. Faced with starvation, they made a radical decision. They would take their chances in the camp of their enemies. When they got there, they found it to be deserted, and so they seized the opportunity to benefit from that circumstance. They entered one of the tents and ate and drank and carried away silver and gold and clothes and hid them. Having done the same in a second tent, their consciences began to bother them. "We're not doing right. This is a day of good news and we are keeping it to ourselves" (2 Kings 7:9).

Their confession summarizes the situation in the lives of many Christians. We have the Good News but are more interested in saving it than sharing it. The programs and priorities of our churches are a reflection of this. Not that we are engaged in activity that is entirely wrong. Surely we want to be good fathers and mothers, develop strong families, and be concerned citizens and Bible-educated Christians. These factors are foundational to effective evangelism. But they cannot take the place of reaching out to our neighbors and friends.

Our goal should be the one defined by a pastor-friend of mine in England: "What ought to be captivating our souls and our minds within the church is: How can I impact the world? How can we be salt and light in a world that's falling apart in despair and confusion and darkness and hopelessness? How can we be involved in fulfilling the great commission and declare that our God is reigning in Jesus and is alive?"[1]

The exhortation of Jesus to "open your eyes and look at the fields! They are ripe for harvest" is as apt for us as it was for His disciples (John 4:35). They were concerned for the physical well-being of Jesus, which clearly was not wrong, but Jesus wanted them to become concerned about the spiritual well-being of the people all around them.

It is all a matter of perspective. On one occasion Jesus and the disciples went by boat to the far shore of Lake Capernaum in search of solitude. By the time they docked the craft, crowds had already gathered. So their rest and relaxation were going to have to wait.

A few verses later the disciples are urging the Master to send the people away. Was that how they felt all along and just couldn't voice their selfish agenda? Jesus had a different response. When He saw the large crowd, He "had compassion on them, because they were like sheep without a shepherd. So he began teaching them many things" (Mark 6:34).

THE GLORY OF GOD

There is nowhere better to begin a study of evangelism than with the first question in the Shorter Scottish Catechism, "What is the chief end of man?" and its answer, "The chief end of man is to glorify God and to enjoy Him forever." Everything we do should be for the glory of God (1 Corinthians 10:31). The overarching objective in the plan of salvation is the glory of God the Father.

In his description of Jesus in Philippians, Paul anticipates a day when "every knee" will bow and "every tongue confess that Jesus Christ is Lord"—and this will be "to the glory of God the Father" (2:10–11). The same emphasis is found in the first chapter of Ephesians. Those whom God has chosen to be His possession have become such "for the praise of his glory" (1:11–14). Until we are convinced of this and our hearts are consumed with a longing for God and His glory, we will be only faintly effective in seeking to address man and his need.

THE COMMAND OF JESUS

Every good soldier wants to please his command-ing officer. Jesus left His disciples with this great stir-ring exhortation:

> All authority in heaven and on earth has been given to me. Therefore go and make disciples of all nations, bap-tizing them in the name of the Father and of the Son and of the Holy Spirit, and teaching them to obey everything I have commanded you. And surely I am with you always, to the very end of the age. (Matthew 28:18–20).

Jesus was not giving a suggestion to consider but a command to obey. We dare not make our feelings the determining factor when it comes to telling others of Jesus. Wesley is reputed to have done so on one occa-sion and was forced to abandon his approach when a significant period of time had elapsed without his hav-ing spoken to anyone about Christ. This is not to say that we should be devoid of a sense of internal com-pulsion (as we shall see) but that, irrespective of how we feel at any given moment, we must recognize that to be a witness for Christ is a duty and a privilege.

THE NEED OF THOSE WHO DO NOT KNOW CHRIST

Those without Christ are "without hope and with-out God in the world" (Ephesians 2:12). Although many of our friends would reject such a description of themselves, from time to time in a variety of ways they may become aware of their need. A lack of fulfillment and sense of alienation is increasingly prevalent in our culture. Boris Becker, the high-profile tennis star, said, "I had won Wimbledon twice before, once as the youngest player. I was rich. I had all the material possessions I needed: money, cars, women, everything, [but] I had no inner peace."[2] When we begin to see our crowded cities through the eyes of Jesus, we will also learn to view the people as sheep without a shepherd.

THE COMPULSION OF CHRIST'S LOVE

"Nothing seals the lips and ties the tongue like the poverty of our own spiritual experience. We say nothing because we have nothing to say."[3] Our witness—good or bad—is the overflow of our lives. One doesn't need to be in the company of a young man in love for very long without becoming aware of his desire to extol his beloved's endearing qualities. In the same way our witness for the Lord Jesus should be the spontaneous and natural consequence of our experience of His love and power in our lives. That was the explanation given by Peter and John of why they preached. "We cannot help speaking about what we have seen and heard" (Acts 4:20). Similarly, Paul declares, "Christ's love compels us" (2 Corinthians 5:14).

There are other motivating factors. We should be stirred by the prospect of the return of Jesus, stirred the Father has promised the nations as His Son's inheritance, and stirred by the desire to hear the Lord's "well done!"

If evangelism is not a passion for the pastor, it will not be a priority for the people. Paul exhorted Timothy to "do the work of an evangelist" (2 Timothy 4:5). The pastor must train his people in evangelism, and he must do evangelism himself. Spurgeon said: "The true gospel minister will have a real yearning over souls something like Rachel when she cried, 'Give me children, or else I die.' So will he cry to God, that he may have his elect born, and brought home to him. And, methinks, every true Christian should be exceedingly earnest in prayer concerning the souls of the ungodly; and when they are so, how abundantly God blesses them and how the church prospers!"[4]

EVANGELISM AS A PURPOSE STATEMENT

It is one thing to feel deeply about an issue and still another to translate how we feel into what we do. It has been said that most churches think they are doing fine because they don't know what they are doing! The purpose statements of many churches are long on clichés and short on understandable and applicable terminology. We have worked hard to reduce the purpose statement of our church to just ten words: "To see unbelieving people become committed followers of Jesus Christ." This is in accord with the concise statement of purpose provided by the apostle Paul in 1 Corinthians 9:19: "To win as many as possible." There was no one more concerned about the growth and maturity of new believers than Paul. From Athens he sent Timothy to Thessalonica "to strengthen and encourage you in your faith" (1 Thessalonians 3:2). "Now we really live, since you are standing firm in the Lord," he said (3:8). He lived in the awareness that there were always more who had never heard, and so he was unashamedly a soul-winner. He would have understood the comment on evangelism made by the late Paul Smith of the People's Church in Toronto: "Why should anyone hear the gospel for a second time when there are still those who have never heard it once?"

Before we include ourselves in this emphasis, let us ask just where the focus of contemporary Christianity in America is to be found. Whether by design or default, we have become "the religious right," with a significant political preoccupation. We are the custodians of virtue and the protectors of freedom and the champions of family and the keepers of promise. But instead of these concerns remaining secondary to the issues of the Gospel, they have taken center stage.

This may seem good, but there is a danger in it. If the church completely retreats from the culture, how is it to impact the culture? We are in danger of setting up a remote counterculture that fails to speak to the world of our neighbors, work associates, and friends. We are cultivating Christians who believe that as long as they are in cozy accountability groups and steer clear of the problem areas, all is well.

But what about an all-consuming passion to see men and women come to faith in Christ? One doesn't need to be a Christian to embrace the emphasis on the family and virtue and political conservatism, but only a Christian will be prepared to challenge the world with the claims of Jesus Christ. The unique danger at this point in history is that we will fail to "contend for the faith that was once for all entrusted to the saints" (Jude 3), but instead succeed in passing on to the coming generation an agenda but not a theology. Without the fixed building blocks of biblical theology, our flimsy constructions will fall flat. Paul makes clear that he is consumed with the thought of winning people to Christ. But what of his strategy?

INTEGRITY AND IMPACT

Paul tells us that he is prepared to modify his habits, adjust his lifestyle, and set aside his preferences "so that by all possible means I might save some" (1 Corinthians 9:22). He is willing to use a great variety of methods so long as they combine maximum integrity with maximum impact. Pursued in this way, becoming "all things to all men" will not be about proclaiming a different message, but about adopting different roles and angles of approach in accordance with the way people differ.

Paul started where people are. When he approached the Jews, he was as Jewish as necessary. If participating in some of their special days and feasts opened a door for the Gospel, he was prepared to do it. He was willing, for example, to have Timothy circumcised (Acts 16:3) and was willing to take part in a purification ceremony in the temple (Acts 21:20–26) even though, we know from Galatians, he was opposed to blending works with grace. In these cases, from one perspective, he put himself "under the law."

When Paul dealt with the Gentiles, he was prepared to ignore religious obligations in order to reach into the world of those who were beyond the pale of religious orthodoxy. And what of "the weak" (1 Corinthians 8)? Well, he stoops to their level. If they need to be starting with the ABCs, that's where he will start. He was prepared to cross a cultural gap rather than shout across it. We must learn from him. We must beware of living in a Christian subculture of cozy gatherings where we speak a foreign language we expect others to learn before they can hear our message.

That does not mean that we should undertake things that God has forbidden just so we can please men. Paul did not allow the culture to determine his strategy or curtail his message. We need to distinguish between the things that are neutral and the things that are clearly wrong. Making such distinctions is often very difficult. That means that if we accept the challenge of building bridges in order to communicate effectively with contemporary paganism, we will have to learn to live with risk.

Adaptability does not mean an inevitable compromise of the message. The fact that some have apparently diluted the Gospel in an attempt to build bridges does not mean that we should cease bridge building and erect fortresses. Rather, we must build according to the Maker's instructions.

SEEKER-SENSITIVE WORSHIP

What about seeker-sensitive worship? Are there only two positions in this debate? Position A defends to the hilt every kind of methodology imaginable in order to make the Gospel palatable. Position B rejects any kind of imaginative approach in sharing the Gospel and describes all who attempt such strategies as compromisers. Perhaps I should enter the discussion with a word of testimony.

Seeker services are not new to me. They were being held in Glasgow, Scotland, when I was a child growing up in the 1950s. They were exciting occasions. About one hour before the service was to begin, a crowd gathered in the open air about a half mile from the building. The object was to attract as many passersby as possible. There were singers and banjo players and a clarinetist who, I was told, before his conversion had been a member of the band on a transatlantic liner. He could play "The Old Rugged Cross" with such skill and pathos that even drunk men in the crowd were reduced to tears.

Interspersed with the music were testimonies from key members of the group. At an appropriate time the gathered crowd would be invited to the second stage of the event, which would take place at the Tent Hall down the street. The makeshift band led the procession down the road and into the auditorium, where cheery-faced ushers provided each one with an empty mug, a small box of food, and a bright red copy of *Redemption Songs*.

With the congregation of some two thousand assembled, the proceedings commenced. An opening hymn and a prayer were followed by the arrival of a squadron of volunteers bearing down on the crowd with the largest teapots ever made. Seated in pews, we juggled the mugs of steaming tea as we ate from our boxes and engaged in happy conversation with our neighbors. Following this feeding of the two thousand, the service began in earnest. Plenty of music. Special selections on the piano and organ—a visiting soloist and sometimes something really wild, such as a man playing melodies on the blunt edge of a large saw. From time to time the speaker had a unique talent, which was demonstrated in the early part of the program and often tied in with the sermon that followed.

It was in this context that I first encountered the chalk artistry of George Sweeting, who was representative of the high caliber of evangelists who used to visit from the United States. The Gospel would be presented with clarity and passion, and an opportunity given to people to respond to the message they had heard. Such opportunities were usually framed by the singing of a hymn.

What did those occasions have in common with contemporary seeker services? They shared a desire to be imaginative and creative in the angle of approach in reaching as many as possible with the Gospel. They also shared a sense of prayerful expectancy that God would work through these means. They were motivated by the needs of men and women without Christ. In what way did they differ from seeker services today?

The primary way they differed was that they were not driven by market analysis to find out what people like and dislike and then cater to that. Contemporary Christian literature is awash with the notion that, in order to be effective and successful, we must respond to market forces. In an earlier generation, such an approach was unheard of. The tactic employed by Paul in Corinth was far closer to the model of the day: "Jesus Christ and him crucified." That was his message. Even though the Corinthians were demanding miracles and wisdom, Paul did not give them what they wanted. Indeed, he continued to supply the one thing they clearly did not want—preaching. He rejected the style and content that was most acceptable in his day.

But surely this threatened the possibility of great results? Didn't he risk failure? Would he not be thought foolish? Yes! But he did not allow that to divert him. He understood that if he employed the eloquent and persuasive oration of the Greek orators and the speculative philosophy of the rationalists, he might capture their attention. But he chose not to do so. He had an unshakable conviction that his responsibility was to bear the name of Christ (Acts 9:15), and he was not about to be sidetracked by paying undue attention to the expectations of his audience. He understood what we seem so slow to learn—that it is not possible to give people what they want to hear and proclaim the message of the Cross at one and the same time.

Does this then mean that any attempt at being imaginative or relevant must be rejected out of hand? No. Being relevant does not mean that we have to depart from the truth. For example, the lyrics of popular songs are often a very real point of contact insofar as they reflect the cries of the human heart. It is no violation of biblical orthodoxy to employ them as a means of introducing the help which is found in Jesus alone, who will give rest for the weary and relief for the burdened.

A similar use may be made of literature. I have already mentioned Jerome K. Jerome's *Three Men in a Boat* and its wonderful description of the emptiness of material possessions. To employ that book may well register in the mind of our listener and provide a bridge over which we can walk with the biblical affirmation: "Godliness with contentment is great gain" (1 Timothy 6:6).

This has absolutely nothing to do with "entertaining people into the kingdom" (as if we could). It is more like what Paul was doing in Athens (Acts 17:22–31). Alister McGrath observes of that incident: "The entire episode illustrates the manner in which Paul is able to exploit the situation of his audience, without compromising the integrity of faith."[5]

CALLED BY HIS GLORY

Paul tells the Corinthian church to "make it [your] goal to please him" (2 Corinthians 5:9). He tells the Ephesians to "find out what pleases the Lord" (Ephesians 5:10). Like the four lepers in 2 Kings, we do not want to keep the good news to ourselves. "The fruit of the righteous is a tree of life, and he who wins souls is wise" (Proverbs 11:30). A major part of that good news is that the victory is already won. The enemy camp is ripe for the plunder, and the gates of hell shall not prevail against the advance. The only question is whether we will be wise by obeying the battle call, winning souls, and living victorious lives—lives that are pleasing to God.

Conclusion

*A*nd so as we gauge our lives by these benchmarks, we come to recognize how important it is to do the basics well most of the time. In service and sacrifice, marriage and ministry, in learning to say "no" to materialism and "yes" to evangelism, our focus is clear. Having been made for His pleasure, we seek to live for His glory.

This calls for consistent endeavor as we work out our salvation with fear and trembling. When we are tempted to conclude that this is "mission impossible," we remind ourselves that "His divine power has given us everything we need for life and godliness" (2 Peter 1:3). We are stirred to renewed faithfulness by the encouragement of the apostle Paul: "Being confident of this, that he who began a good work in you will carry it on to completion until the day of Christ Jesus" (Philippians 1:6).

For each of us there will be a last time for every journey. We will eventually strike camp and head for our permanent home. But as the future creeps in at the rate of sixty seconds per minute, we need to ensure that our "earthly tents" are secured by these biblical principles which glorify God and stabilize us. When our desires, decisions, aspirations, and affections are increasingly governed by our prior determination to please God, then as we run the race set out before us, we may, like Eric Liddell, feel *His* pleasure!

> To him who is able to keep you from falling and to present you before his glorious presence without fault and with great joy—to the only God our Savior be glory, majesty, power and authority, through Jesus Christ our Lord, before all ages, now and forevermore! (Jude 24–25)

NOTES

Introduction: The Priority of God in a World of Self

1. John Stott, *Romans: God's Good News for the World*, (Downers Grove, Ill.: InterVarsity, 1994).
2. David F. Wells, *God in the Wasteland: The Reality of Truth in a World of Fading Dreams* (Grand Rapids: Eerdmans: 1994), 93.

Chapter 1: Spiritual Fitness in a Flabby Generation

1. Robert Robinson (1745–1790), "Come, Thou Fount of Every Blessing." Text from *Worship and Service Hymnal* (Chicago: Hope,1957). Public domain.
2. Annie Johnson Flint (1862–1932), "He Giveth More Grace." Text from *Sing His Praise* (Springfield, Mo.: Gospel, 1991). Lyrics in the public domain.

Chapter 2: Prayer That Is Larger Than Ourselves

1. William Walford (1772–1850), "Sweet Hour of Prayer." Text from *Worship and Service Hymnal* (Chicago: Hope, 1957). Public domain.
2. Peter Deyneka, *A Song in Siberia* (Elgin, Ill.: David C. Cook, 1977), 58.
3. Derek Prime, *Practical Prayer: The Why and How of Prayer* (London: Hodder & Stoughton, 1985), 101.
4. Adapted from Derek Prime, *Practical Christianity*.

Chapter 3: Sacrifice: Wholehearted Commitment to God's Kingdom

1. *Newsweek*, 3 July 1978, © 1978. Newsweek, Inc. All rights reserved. Reprinted by permission.
2. J. White, "For Me to Live Is Christ." Text from *Youth Praise II* (London: Kings Way).
3. Dietrich Bonhoeffer, *The Cost of Discipleship* (New York: Macmillan, 1963), 79.
4. Epictetus, *Discourses* I.16.20f, quoted in John Stott, *Romans: God's Good News for the World* (Downers Grove, Ill.: InterVarsity, 1994), 321.
5. Stott, *Romans*, 322.

Chapter 6: Suffering: Pleasing God When the Wheels Fall Off

1. William Cowper (1731–1800), "God Moves in a Mysterious Way." Text from *Hymns of Faith* (London: Scripture Union, 1964). Public domain.
2. John R. W. Stott, *The Cross of Christ* (Downers Grove, Ill.: InterVarsity, 1986), 239.
3. Richard Greenham, in *The Golden Treasury of Puritan Quotations*, comp. I. D. E. Thomas (Chicago: Moody, 1975; Edinburgh: Banner of Truth Trust, 1977), 13.
4. Fanny J. Crosby (1820–1915), "A Few More Marchings." Text from *Redemption Hymns* (London: Pickering & Ingles). Public domain.
5. Alexander Smellie, *Men of the Covenant: The Story of the Scottish Church in the Years of Persecution* (London: Andrew Melrose, 1903), 275.
6. Abraham Wright, in *The Golden Treasury of Puritan Quotations*, 17.

Chapter 7: The Narrow Way: Never Did a Heedless Person Lead a Holy Life

1. Alister McGrath, *Bridge-building: Effective Christian Apologetics* (London: Inter-Varsity, 1992), 148.
2. William Gurnall, in *The Golden Treasury of Puritan Quotations*, comp. I. D. E. Thomas (Chicago: Moody, 1975; Edinburgh: Banner of Truth Trust, 1977), 140.

Chapter 8: Intellectualism and Materialism: Chasing After the Wind

1. Alister McGrath, *Bridge-building: Effective Christian Apologetics* (London: Inter-Varsity, 1992), 51.
2. Malcolm Muggeridge, *Jesus Rediscovered* (London: Hodder & Stoughton).
3. Tony Hancock, in *Famous Last Words*, comp. Jonathon Green (London: Omnibus, 1979), 118.
4. Robert Burns, "Tam o' Shanter."
5. Jerome K. Jerome, *Three Men in a Boat* (1889; reprint, Harmondsworth, England: Penguin, 1957).
6. Jerome, *Three Men in a Boat*, 26–27.

Chapter 10: Evangelism: The Necessity of Bringing Others to Christ

1. Jim Graham, quoted in "Passing Through," *LBC Review* (London Bible College), Autumn 1994, 11.
2. Alister McGrath, *Bridge-building: Effective Christian Apologetics* (London: Inter-Varsity, 1992), 20.
3. John Stott, *Romans: God's Good News for the World* (Downers Grove, Ill.: InterVarsity, 1994).
4. Charles Haddon Spurgeon, *Autobiography*, 1:329.
5. McGrath, *Bridge-building*, 49.